Your Season of Significance

I sincerely hope your team wins the state championship this year. Chances are you won't. How's that for motivation? The question is: How can you play beyond the scoreboard and lead your team to a season of significance regardless of your record? Am I saying your record is not important? No. Winning is great. I love to win, and I don't like losing. It's possible that using the ideas in this book may help your team win a few additional contests this year.

As a team captain, you will have the opportunity and the responsibility to lead your team to a season of significance, regardless of your record. *Playing Beyond the Scoreboard*

means looking at more than just wins and losses. It's about looking at the entire experience of athletics and being a leader as a building block to the future. The lessons you learn can last an entire lifetime.

About
the
Author

Craig Hillier has been speaking to teens since 1990, and he speaks to more than 75,000 young people each year. His high-energy programs and contagious enthusiasm captivate audiences throughout the United States. In addition to leadership keynotes and school assemblies, Craig focuses his efforts on student leadership training. His programs are upbeat, fun, and educational. Craig was awarded the Outstanding Young Alumni Award from Mankato State University and is a CSP (certified speaking professional) with the National Speakers Association. He also is the author of *How to Step Up as a Teen Leader*. He lives in Lakeville, Minnesota, with his wife Kelly and two children, Derrick and Abigayle.

PLAYING BEYOND THE SCOREBOARD

A Team Captain's Guide to a Season of Significance

A Winning Edge Seminars Publication
10968 203rd Street West
Lakeville, MN 55044
(952) 985-5885 • (800) 446-3343 • fax (952) 985-5886
email: WinningE@aol.com
web site: www.craighillier.com

ISBN 0-9657828-5-9

Dedication

To Kelly, Abigayle and Derrick. Thanks for letting
me do what I get to do. I love you very much.

Acknowledgments

Special thanks to Steve Potts and Jolene Roehlkepartain for editing; Greg Wimmer, the cover designer; Kelly Hillier, Chris Hillier, Eric Chester, Bill Cordes, John Behrends, Scott Monson, Rick Bouchard, Terry Kadrmas, and Tim Knower for content ideas. It was a great team to work with!

Contents

Part 1: On Your Mark

Part 2: Get Set

How to Use this Book

According to Webster's dictionary, significance is defined as "meaningful, important." Success is defined as a "favorable result, becoming famous." Significance is about creating lasting, important memories and lessons while success is about the end result or team record. Ideally, your season would be both significant and successful. I can't guarantee you a successful season, but I can predict you'll have a significant season by using the material in this book.

This book is a working manual for your season. Keep it in a place you can refer to often. Hopefully this will be a resource you will toss in a box of high school stuff when you graduate. Then in future years when you think about some of the highlights of high school you will look at the book and it will rekindle some incredible memories.

A Manual on Leadership

Up until now there have been few resources on becoming a strong team leader. *Playing Beyond the Scoreboard* examines the ins and outs of team leadership. You'll find out what to do and what to stay away from in the upcoming season. Obviously, it's impossible to cover every aspect of the season, just as it's impossible to highlight every sport in high school. Yet this book is for you—no matter which sport you play. Throughout the book, you'll read specific references to various sports. If your sport isn't mentioned, it doesn't mean that it's not worthwhile.

As you read this book, you may find some examples that don't apply to your sport. For example, you may read about "games" when you play "matches." Don't get caught up in looking for the exception to every rule or the exception to a principle. You'll probably always find an exception to every idea, no matter how solid the idea is. Read the information and then adapt the information to your sport or situation.

You'll also notice that sometimes you'll be reading examples about guys while other times you'll see examples about girls. Instead of constantly using the "he or she" and the "him or her" approach, this book alternates gender examples so that the book is easier to read. Don't be tempted to skip over all the examples about the opposite sex because the entire book is written for you. Everything applies to you.

This book is divided into four parts:

- On Your Mark

- Get Set

- Go!

- Instant Replay

The "On Your Mark" section stretches your mind and helps you warm up to the dynamics of leadership. You will learn about ten myths of leadership, the commitments of a captain, and how to examine your own leadership style.

The "Get Set" section focuses on preparing for the season. You will have an opportunity to learn about creating team chemistry and developing a team vision. In addition, preseason questionnaires have been designed to help you set goals for the upcoming season. This process will prove to be challenging and rewarding.

The "Go!" section gets you out of the blocks as the season begins. This section deals with some of the highs and lows a typical season brings. You will discover ten ways to set a positive tone with your team and the impact drugs and alcohol have on a team and individual performance. You will learn strategies for working through conflict, developing sportsmanship and various tips that will be valuable throughout the season.

Finally, the "Instant Replay" section gives you ideas on how to look back over your season. You will find out ways to appreciate your coach and evaluate your team. This section also includes three appendices, one on resources, another on FUNdraisers, and another on inspiring sports quotes. At the end of the book, you'll find "About Your Season," which has a place for you to put your picture and record some of the significant events and memories of your season.

This book is filled with tips, tactics, and strategies that allow you to fully understand the role of a successful team leader. You'll find out the best strategies for dealing with teammates and coaches. The information in this book comes from my work with thousands of high school leaders throughout the United States. Several topnotch coaches have been interviewed on team leadership. Hundreds of surveys have been compiled from coaches and captains. You are receiving the wisdom from thousands of people who have been in your leadership position.

You're on Your Way

Team Captain. It sounds good doesn't it? You probably always wanted this position. Now that you have it, you may be wondering the same thing I was as a team captain.

Now what? My training as a captain went something like this, "Okay, you're the captain, and the coaching staff is expecting great things from you." That was it! Most of the lessons on being a captain I learned the hard way. I'm hoping this information will allow you to avoid the pitfalls and enjoy the pinnacles of leadership.

So team captain, get on your mark and proceed to chapter one!

PART 1

ON YOUR MARK

CHAPTER 1

What makes it worth it?

Do I have what it takes to be a captain? What if I mess up? Will I be as good as last year's captain? How will I do in this role? One or all of these questions may be burning in your mind as you approach the upcoming season as a captain. Rest assured, doubting yourself is common. As you begin your new role, it's okay to feel a little anxious. That anxiety will push you to prepare yourself for the challenge.

Becoming a team captain is an honor and a privilege. The team will be looking for you to be an example and to provide guidance when the season is going awesome—and when it's about to fall apart. If you can learn to work positively with others as a teenager and deal with the tricky situations involved in leading, it will be incredible to see what you can accomplish in the future.

Being a team leader is an awesome experience. I know you're ready to get into the information in the book so let's get started by dispelling ten myths of leading. Remember, the word myth means a *false* or *fictitious* belief or story.

Ten Myths of Being a Captain

Myth 1: You are still part of the "gang." When you accepted the role of team captain you also gave up being a part of the gang. At times, this is a challenging spot to be in. The coach is expecting you to be a shining example of a strong work ethic and discipline while your teammates and friends may be expecting you to cut them a break when they are slacking off and not working hard. Many times, you are going to feel like a rubber band being pulled in two different directions. The best captains get comfortable with being pulled in two directions. The key is to stretch without snapping.

Myth 2: The best players = the best leaders. Too often it is assumed that if you're a great player you instantly become a great team leader. Leadership skills and athletic skills are vastly different. Leadership is about *people skills* while athletic skills typically focus on *physical talent.* It's no secret most of the great coaches in sports were average players at best. However, an average athlete with excellent leadership ability can lead a team to an incredible season. Sometimes the most talented athletes can't understand why every-

one doesn't have the same ability they have. Therefore, they have a difficult time communicating with team members who are not at their same skill level. In a crucial situation, these types of leaders take it upon themselves to ensure a victory. If they were a little more objective, however, a different plan may be more effective. Don't get me wrong; if you are the best player on the team you have an excellent opportunity to lead. If you have the physical talent and apply the principles in this book, look out!

Myth 3: You must be loud to be a leader. A good friend of mine once said, "Don't confuse the loud with the strong." It seems there are a lot of people who are very loud but don't say anything of value. Some leaders are gifted at getting a team fired up with their words prior to a game. For others, getting up in front of the team and trying to give a "pump up" talk will not work. However, they lead by example. They may only say a few words, but their words are so valuable and thought out everyone takes them to heart. Both loud leaders and quiet leaders can be powerful team captains.

Myth 4: Leaders must be popular. Colin Powell in his "Leadership Primer" program says, "Good leadership involves responsibility to the welfare of the group, which means that some people will get angry at your actions and decisions. It's inevitable if you're honorable. Trying to get everyone to like you is a sign of mediocrity: you'll avoid the tough decisions, you'll avoid confronting the people who need to be confronted."

Great team captains get comfortable being uncomfortable. To be effective, you're going to have to make some difficult decisions. Remember, it's impossible to get everyone's approval.

Myth 5: You're the boss. If you're not careful, the title of team captain can go to your head. You were elected or selected to lead the team, not boss the team. Bosses usually just tell others what to do and then watch the progress.

Great leaders may give several ideas and then join in to ensure success. Taking a "let's go do it" versus a "you go do it" will demonstrate you not only have the heart to lead but that you are willing to carry out your plans and strategies.

Myth 6: Captains are the only leaders on the team. The best leaders understand they need to engage as many players as they can into leadership roles. They don't attempt to have all the answers to every situation. They are willing to ask for input from others. Think of your team as a flock of geese who fly in a V formation to become more aerodynamic. The lead goose is not always the lead goose. Geese usually rotate being in front. You can take the same approach. It's important to help others develop as leaders. Chances are you are going to be a captain for one, maybe two years. By developing some of the younger teammates, you are helping to predict a season of significance for the people who will be playing in the next few years.

Myth 7: Captains can't mess up. My friend Bill Cordes and I share a powerful statement in our live presentations you can use for the rest of your life: *Mistakes are great moments.* Are all mistakes great moments? No. Is getting drunk and crashing your car a great moment? No. Is bringing a weapon to school a great moment? No. Is calling in a bomb threat a great moment? No.

Mistakes become great moments when we mess up in pursuit of something that's important. When you mess up, turn away and celebrate it. You just figured out what not to do! Don't expect or even pursue perfection. Deal with mistakes and then move on. When you are leading a team, you are putting yourself in a position to fail occasionally. If you are not making a few mistakes every day, you are not human. Some people play life so safe they seldom make mistakes. However, by not attempting something new or different, people who play it safe are making a huge mistake because they will never get a chance to see what they could become because they never tried something new. Be willing to stick your neck out and take a risk daily. If you have a great moment, smile, learn the lesson, and then move on.

Myth 8: Respect can be demanded not earned. In today's world, respect is seldom granted. Team leaders who constantly listen to coaches and teammates and avoid negative verbal assaults while encouraging teammates can create a climate of respect. *Titles don't equal respect.* Connecting with others creates respect. Don't expect people to bow when you enter the room. The title of captain is granted. Earning it means working for it every day.

Myth 9: Last year = this year. It's tempting to let last year's season affect this year's approach. Don't fall into that trap. If your team won a state champi-

onship last year, great; but this team is made up of different people. You will have to work even harder to attain a championship this year. No one is handed a title because of last year's performance. On the other hand, if last year was a disaster, this is the time to turn it around. Don't let the previous year become a shadow for this season.

Myth 10: You're indispensable. Bill Cordes shares an interesting story about a team leader on a football team. T.C. was a star athlete, but his work ethic was weak. A new coach was hired and expected a strong effort from everyone. T.C. thought he was above putting in that kind of effort so he decided to quit the team. He thought the team would struggle without him and soon team members would beg for his return. But that didn't happen. The team went on and won a state championship without him. Could you imagine sitting in the stands knowing you could have been a part of a team like that? Everyone can be replaced!

The Truth about Being a Captain

Now that you know the myths of being a captain, what about the truth? The truth is: It's going to be a memorable, valuable experience. One you will never forget. You will have the chance to really make a difference this season. Captains have the opportunity to help teammates reach beyond their potential. The truth is: A team will never have a season of significance without great leadership. You're the one who has been selected or elected to take this position.

The chapter title asks, "What makes it worth it?" I think Tom Hanks, in the movie "A League of Their Own," answers this question.

"A League of Their Own" illustrates the difficult part of keeping a team together while facing several obstacles. At a pivotal point in the movie, the team leader of the women's professional baseball team has had enough and wants to quit. Tom Hanks, who plays the coach of the team, asks, "Why do you want to quit?" The woman replies, "It just got too hard." Hanks, in this defining moment, pauses to reflect and responds, "It's the hard part that makes it worth it."

This same principle applies to being a captain. It's not going to be an easy, uneventful, smooth ride. You may run into situations where you wonder why you wanted to be a team leader. It's not uncommon to doubt your leadership ability. You may think it would have just been easier to be a team member versus trying to lead the team. As you face these situations, remember the words of Tom Hanks, *"It's the hard part that makes it worth it."*

"

Leadership

"The best leaders know how to elevate some people, calm some people, and create one beating heart."

— Paul "Bear" Bryant

"What I've learned in my years as a competitive wheelchair athlete is this—what separates a winner from the rest of the pack is not raw talent or physical ability; instead, it is the drive and dedication to work hard every single day, and the heart to go after your dream, no matter how unattainable others think it is."

— Linda Mastandrea

"

CAPTAIN'S CLIPBOARD

Ten Myths of Being a Captain

1. You are still part of the "gang."

2. The best players = the best leaders.

3. You must be loud to be a leader.

4. Leaders must be popular.

5. You're the boss.

6. Captains are the only leaders on the team.

7. Captains can't mess up.

8. Respect can be demanded, not earned.

9. Last year = this year.

10. You're indispensable.

CHAPTER 2

A Captain's Commitment

Pat Riley, a professional basketball coach once said, "You are either in or you're out, there are no in-betweens." The same principle applies to being a team leader. So are you in or are you out? By being "in" you are totally committing yourself to your coach, team and sport.

I've surveyed coaches, captains, and players regarding the personal qualities they looked for in team captains. The responses were fundamental; carrying them out is far from fundamental.

From the research, eight key qualities emerged. By committing to the following personal qualities you are setting the stage to play beyond the scoreboard. Consider the list as a checklist for your level of commitment.

Key #1: Passion

If you wanted to become a captain to get your picture in the yearbook or have your name announced during the introduction of each game or match, surrender your title now. I'm serious! Let someone else take the leadership reins because you won't be effective if you're searching for glory. If you wanted to be a captain because of a strong passion to guide a team, however, you're in the right place. Great captains have a passion for the sport and being around their teammates. They are not shy about showing their enthusiasm and love for the sport.

Key #2: Trustworthiness

After the coach walks out the door, do you mock or verbally slam him? If someone on your team shares some confidential family information, do you spread it to the rest of the team and then to the entire school?

Being trustworthy is about keeping some information confidential. If someone confides in you and asks you to keep a secret, you're being trustworthy if you don't tell anyone else—not even your best friend. Trustworthy team leaders know a lot of information about people, but they don't spread it around.

There are a few times, however, when you shouldn't keep a secret. If someone shares information about hurting him- or herself—or hurting others, you must tell someone who can help. Who do you tell? A trustworthy adult. That person could be a coach, a teacher, a parent, or a counselor. A trustworthy adult will know what to do.

So what about you? Can you keep information confidential when it won't be harmful to others? When there is a threat of someone being hurt, do you feel comfortable communicating the issue with an adult? If so, you're a trustworthy captain.

Key #3: Knowledge

Referees and officials say they are often amazed at how many athletes don't know the rules of the game. Most athletes learn how to play the game through experience (by playing) or watching others play. You can learn a lot that way, but there are several rules you'll never learn unless you open up a rulebook.

Many players and captains have never read the rulebook for their sport. Why? They think the coach or athletic director has explained all the rules. But if you're going to develop true knowledge for the game, it's vital to get a current rulebook and read it cover to cover.

Chances are when you read the rule book, most of it will be review. I'll guarantee you'll learn something you don't know. Maybe a new rule has been adapted for the new season. Most sports have rule changes every year.

If you know the rules, you will have credibility with an official during a game. If you know what you're talking about, you can approach an official with confidence and ask for clarification or interpretation on a call or decision.

I remember watching a professional golf tournament where the golfers resumed play after a two-hour rain delay. A famous golfer hit his tee shot under a tree. The only way to hit the next shot without touching a branch with his club was to get down on both of his knees. Because it was so damp after the rain, he put a towel on the ground so his pants wouldn't get dirty as he kneeled.

He hit a miraculous shot that landed on the green. The crowd went crazy. However, there was a problem. The PGA rules stated that there could not be any item placed under a golfer to improve the golfer's shot. The officials considered the towel a device that would improve his shot since the golfer would be less likely to slip during the back swing.

The golfer was given a two-shot penalty and came in second that day. The mistake cost him more than $100,000 and the title. Not knowing the rules is costly.

Key #4: Organization

Who are you playing next week? What time is practice today? Where is the fundraiser going to be held? When you're a cap-

tain you have to know what's going on and when it's going to happen. Many coaches are amazed at the lack of organization their team captains possess. If you're a teen leader, you probably have a million things to keep track of in your life. It's almost impossible to keep all of them in your head. If you do, chances are you are going to miss some important events.

While it may not seem cool to carry a calendar or planner, it is essential to get one prior to the season starting. It doesn't have to be a monster three ring binder with 400 pages in it. Go to an office products store and select a planner that fits your life style. Several have been designed especially for teenagers.

Once you've selected a planner or calendar, write all the dates of games and contests immediately. Some of the information will need to be added throughout the season. If you're not on top of the schedule, you will look bad and your teammates and coaches may begin to doubt your commitment.

Key #5: Honesty

When Jennifer Capriati was a teenage tennis player, she was competing in the championship match in a major tournament. Late in the match, her opponent hit the ball deep, and Jennifer decided not to return it. The judge called the ball out.

But Jennifer knew that the ball was really in. She told the line judge, and the line judge reversed the call. Jennifer went on to lose the match that day, however, she won the hearts of everyone watching. She had the courage to be honest. What would you have done in her position?

Teammates, fans, and coaches are watching what you do all the time, but they watch you even closer in crucial situations. Captains who play beyond the scoreboard understand they must be honest even in the most difficult situations. Even when it means losing.

As you continue to grow, the challenge to be honest won't get any easier. If honesty is just your normal way of approaching life, it will become your second nature to state the truth. Too often, people shade the truth and then they have to try to remember what they said. When you are honest, you don't have to remember what you said because it was the truth. Successful team captains are honest—no matter what.

Key #6: Listening

Hearing and listening are two different things. You can hear a coach give an instruction, but did you really listen? In Hugh O'Brian's book: *Visionary Leadership*, he outlines three "Rs" to listening. These strategies are valuable for your season and throughout your life.

- **Repeat** the information you just heard in either exact (if the message is short) or paraphrased form. This allows the person to validate, correct, or add to the message you received. Also, knowing that it is your task to repeat the information, you will probably pay closer attention to what the person is saying.

- **Respond** to the person while she is communicating with you. To really convey to the person that you are with her, you need to respond both verbally and nonverbally. Respond verbally by repeating the message you heard and requesting additional information. Respond nonverbally by making eye contact, nodding, and showing interest in the person who is talking to you.

• **Request** more information from the person you are communicating with. You'll get more complete and detailed information, which is essential for effective leaders. Sometimes you'll even discover that the main message emerges after you ask questions.

Key #7: Flexibility

Let's assume you have played a certain position on the team since you were in middle school. Now the coach is asking you to play a different position. Maybe another player has become much better in the off season and suddenly that player is getting more playing time then you. Maybe a new student moves to your school who is a great talent and will make a strong contribution to the team.

How do you respond? Are you flexible enough to give the new person or position a try? Or do you become stubborn and refuse to adapt?

Flexibility is a must for team captains. It demonstrates you are willing to put the team's needs in front of your own. This won't happen without some internal pain. Sometimes you will have to put your pride aside and look at the big picture of leadership.

Key #8: Caring

In my first book, *How to Step Up as a Teen Leader and Still Keep Your Friends*, I outlined a formula that has been effective for thousands of teen leaders. By using this formula (called CARE), you will create a positive environment with your teammates and coaches.

- **Compliment.** Great leaders are quick to compliment and slow to criticize. When you see a player have a breakthrough, try to be the first one to congratulate them. Most people let their ego or petty jealousy get in the way of giving compliments. Make sure your compliments are honest, sincere, and given out frequently and freely.

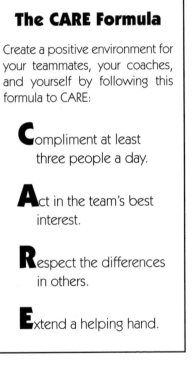

The CARE Formula

Create a positive environment for your teammates, your coaches, and yourself by following this formula to CARE:

Compliment at least three people a day.

Act in the team's best interest.

Respect the differences in others.

Extend a helping hand.

- **Act in the team's best interest.** It's easy to get caught up in thinking about "me" instead of "we." One thing is for sure, when "me" becomes more important than "we," you and your team will struggle. Sacrifice for the good of the team and you will see others do the same.

- **Respect the differences in others.** Most of us would admit to judging someone before we really knew them. Then, after spending some time with them, we found our initial judgment way off or unfair. The lesson is simple; don't judge until you really know them. Even after you know someone, be wise enough to withhold judgment and attempt to accept people for who they are, not what you think they should be. Unfortunately there are still a few narrow-minded people who judge others by their life circumstances or race. Even when you respect the differences in others, you may find people who don't respect you or your teammates. When this happens, it's tempting to become judgmental. You just see things differently from this person. Treat others with respect even if others don't treat you that way.

- **Extend a helping hand.** Is one of your teammates struggling with a slap shot or hurdling technique? Is there someone in your neighborhood who is trying to learn the sport you are captain for? Take the time to extend a helping hand. My son, who is currently in elementary school,  loves it when high students stop for a few minutes and help him on his basketball lay ups on our driveway. Every day you have an opportunity to extend a helping hand. Identify those opportunities and stretch yourself to help. There is no greater feeling in the world than helping someone out.

This CARE formula works wonders. I received an e-mail from a young man who attended one of my leadership programs as a sophomore. He wrote this formula down and committed to using it every day of his life. After using the formula daily, he decided to run for student body president. The school he attended had 2,200 students in grades 10-12. When the results were tallied, this young man received 70% of the votes. It was the largest landslide victory in the school's history. As his e-mail to me stated, he never would have been able to get that many votes without using the CARE formula and making it his second nature.

Eight Key Leadership Qualities

1. Passion

2. Trustworthiness

3. Knowledge

4. Organization

5. Honesty

6. Listening

7. Flexibility

8. Caring

So, Are You In?

Now it's time to identify which qualities are your strengths and which ones need an extra boost. Take the questionnaire, "Eight Key Leadership Qualities" on page 24.

After you finish, look at your results. How did you do? Are you so *passionate* about your sport that it's difficult to keep you quiet? Can people *trust* you when they're not with you? Have you taken the time to develop your *knowledge* about the rules of your sport? Are your *organization* skills strong? Is *honesty* a daily practice? Did you really *listen* to the message being delivered? Can you be *flexible* during challenging times? Do you really *care* about your teammates?

If you're "in," you'll continue to work on these eight key qualities until they become second nature. The next chapter will help you focus on connecting with others.

" Key Qualities

On Passion
"The most important thing is to love your sport. Never do it to please someone else—it has to be yours. That is all that will justify the hard work needed to achieve success. Compete against yourself, not others for that is truly your best competition."

—Peggy Fleming Jenkins

"High school sports: where lessons of life are still being learned and where athletes still compete for the love of the game and their teammates."

—Michael Powers

On Flexibility
"I don't need to be the number one on the team. This is what I train for day in and day out. I am the support player. If I need to hit, pitch, run, whatever—I will do it. If everything was going to be about me, I think I'd quit."

—Michele Smith

On Caring
"A group becomes a team where each member is sure enough of himself and his/her contributions to praise the skills of the others."

—Norman Shidle

"

CAPTAIN'S CLIPBOARD

Eight Key Leadership Qualities

On the next page, evaluate yourself with each of the eight key leadership qualities. Checkmark one box for each quality that best describes where you're at right now.

Eight Key Leadership Qualities

Evaluate yourself with each of these eight key leadership qualities. Checkmark one box for each quality that best describes where you're at right now.

Key Quality	Totally True	Mostly True	Somewhat True	Never True
1. Passionate — I am enthusiastic about my sport, and I can't stop talking about it.	❏	❏	❏	❏
2. Trustworthy — When people tell me their secrets, I don't tell others.	❏	❏	❏	❏
3. Knowledgeable — I know all the rules of the sport I play, and I have read the rule book.	❏	❏	❏	❏
4. Organized — I know what's going on, when things are going to happen, and I keep track of this information in a planner or calendar.	❏	❏	❏	❏
5. Honesty — I always tell the truth, even when it isn't easy.	❏	❏	❏	❏

Key Quality	Totally True	Mostly True	Somewhat True	Never True
6. Listening — When others talk to me, I *repeat* the information I've heard, I *respond* to the person while the person is talking to me, and I *request* more information.	❏	❏	❏	❏
7. Flexibility — I put the team's needs in front of my own and give new people and new positions a try, when necessary.	❏	❏	❏	❏
8. Caring — I follow the CARE formula of *complimenting* others, *acting* in the team's best interest, *respecting* differences, and *extending* a helping hand.	❏	❏	❏	❏

When you're finished, look at the boxes you've checked. What are your strengths? What are your weaknesses?

Now go back and place a star next to the one quality that is the easiest for you. Circle the one that is the most challenging for you. Commit to making all eight of these qualities a top priority.

CHAPTER 3
Connecting as a Captain

Anthony Robbins, a well-known speaker and author says, "The quality of our lives will be determined by the quality of our communication." As a captain, you must have the ability to connect with your coach and with the players. Connecting means creating a true understanding of viewpoints, attitudes, and opinions.

Have you ever had a conversation with someone who seemed to be on the same mental wavelength as you? You probably said to yourself, "Yes, they get it. They understand me. They understand what I believe." When you connect, you and the other person "get it."

Identifying Your Leadership Style

This chapter is designed to help you make a strong connection with people. By understanding different approaches and styles, you become a people magnet. Others will be drawn to you. It's almost impossible to move a group of people in a positive direction unless they are close to you. They become close to you by creating an understanding.

There are four different leadership styles that I've adapted from the Team Dynamics Style® created by Peer Power Communication in Rochester, Minnesota. As you examine each style, determine which style is most like you. Place a number one at the top of that page. Consider which leadership style is second most like you. Place a number two at the top of that page. Then figure out which style fits you the least. Place a number four at the top of that page. This is important information in your journey to connecting with the team.

Page left blank intentionally

Togetherness Style

Characteristics
- Big hearted
- Consistent
- Reliable
- Loyal
- Keeps others involved
- Strong work ethic
- Wants projects in a step-by-step process
- Takes a lot to make them vent their frustrations

Communication Process
1. Listens
2. Evaluates
3. Decides on a response
4. Responds with sensitivity
5. Re-evaluates

Motivating Factors
- Providing support or service to others
- Working cooperatively with others
- Predictable, constant environment
- Quality and accuracy are rewarded
- Verbal or written recognition
- Feelings acknowledged
- Others express their appreciation

Demotivating Factors
- Constant change
- Having to become aggressive with others

- Working all by themselves
- Forced to make a decision immediately
- Lack of appreciation
- Forced to think only objectively and not consider other people's feelings
- Broken promises
- Being publicly embarrassed

Challenges

- Making decisions
- Standing up for their feelings
- Unclear directions or vision
- Saying "no" when others ask for help
- Voicing their opinion after being rejected

Conflict Management

- Tends to avoid interpersonal aggression
- Peacekeeper with others
- Becomes emotional
- Becomes rigid
- Withdraws to plan response
- May become defensive
- May withdraw
- May give in to avoid looking bad or losing approval

Areas of Improvement

- Increase flexibility; go with the flow
- Ask clarifying questions
- Share ideas after initial rejection
- Vent frustrations

Enterpriser Style

Characteristics
- Big-picture perspective
- Task oriented
- Takes action
- Loves to lead
- Hates to lose
- Gets things done
- Hard worker
- Unafraid of change
- Thrives on pressure
- Highly confident
- Speaks openly and boldly

Communication Process
1. Listens selectively
2. Evaluates rapidly
3. Responds
4. Briefly re-evaluates

Motivating Factors
- Having control over situations
- Directing other's actions
- Speaking openly and boldly
- Achieving results based on the ends, not the means of accomplishing them
- Verbal recognition
- Situations where creativity can be tapped
- Performing under pressure
- A constantly changing environment

Demotivating Factors
- Appearing soft or weak
- Situations requiring routine, predictable behavior
- Having to outline a task in a step-by-step format
- When others take conflict personally
- When change takes too long
- Started but not completed projects
- People who withhold feelings or thoughts

Challenges
- Explanations can be vague
- Can appear to be insensitive to others
- Can appear to be closed minded to other's ideas
- Listening all the way through
- Getting off track

Conflict Management
- Takes a direct, aggressive approach
- Creates win/lose outcomes
- May appear to be mad when simply airing thoughts
- Uses their authority position to a supreme advantage
- Increases the level of aggression rapidly
- Attempts to try to clear the air in one meeting

Areas of Improvement
- Get others involved
- Listen to all available options
- Treat others with respect
- Make sure others see your vision
- Stay composed

Analyzer Style

Characteristics
- Big planner
- Approaches things logically
- Thinks it through
- Wants all the information
- Step-by-step thinkers
- May prefer to work independently
- Quality conscious
- Writes their thoughts on paper
- High standards
- Focuses on facts

Communication Process
1. Listens
2. Evaluates
3. Re-evaluates
4. Responds
5. Justifies

Motivating Factors
- Performing to their own standards
- Controlling facts that affect performance
- Being right
- Logical, systematic approach to tasks
- Solving problems no one else has been able to solve
- Thought-provoking discussions
- Surrounded by others who stay on task

Demotivating Factors
- Being held responsible to someone else's standards
- Having to make an immediate decision

- Situations where a subjective, personal response is required
- Rules or expectations that constantly change
- When their quality is not appreciated
- False recognition
- Others who goof off during crunch times
- Discussions that go off task

Challenges
- Accepting others whose standards are lower
- Making a choice with an adequate amount of information
- Spur-of-the-moment decisions
- Finding how a project or an idea won't work
- Taking action

Conflict Management
- Remains calm
- Overpowers others with facts and logic
- Requests extensive instructions when faced with new situations
- May withdraw to decide on a response strategy
- Quietly resists
- Withholds information
- Becomes defensive. May say, "That's not how it was explained to me."

Areas of Improvement
- Increase flexibility; go with the flow
- Find a way to make a project or an idea work
- Explain why the details are important
- Combine your idea with others

Motivator Style

Characteristics
- Big mouth
- Enthusiastic
- High energy
- Likes to talk
- Dislikes details
- Likes people
- Optimistic
- Emotional
- Articulate
- Likes catchy phrases
- Works well with others

Communication Process
1. Listens selectively
2. Responds impulsively
3. Evaluates rapidly
4. Responds again

Motivating Factors
- Positive interaction with others
- Opportunities to verbalize thoughts and feelings
- Verbal or written recognition awards
- New challenges
- Rewards for achieving goals
- Frequent change
- Competition
- Inspiring others to achieve results

Demotivating Factors
- Situations where others may react with hostility
- Extensive detail
- Pessimistic surroundings or people
- Repetitive situations that don't change
- Lack of flexibility in others
- Working alone
- Lack of recognition
- People who are always serious

Challenges
- Overuses enthusiasm
- Lack of organization skills
- Has several projects going on with only a few that are complete
- Actions may not be thought all the way through

Conflict Management
- Avoids open, direct conflict
- Attacks others personally
- Seeks revenge by persuading others to take their side
- May seek revenge indirectly
- Becomes emotional
- Minimizes negative information
- Takes criticism or conflict personally
- May openly joke after the conflict is over but is still upset

Areas of Improvement
- Plan things through to the end
- Concentrate on completion
- Focus
- Listen all the way
- Get beyond the idea and take action

Understanding Your Leadership Style

Now that you've had a chance to view each of the styles, one of the four probably strikes you as being *most* like you. Obviously each person is made up of all four styles, but typically there is one style that is most like you. It's not uncommon for people to feel they are close or tied between one style and another. If you are in that situation, try to determine the one that slightly edges out the other style and circle the style that is most like you on the page titled, "Your Leadership Style." That's the one you rated as number one.

The supporting role is the style that is next most like you. Circle the style that you rated as number two.

The style that is least like you is known as the villain role. As you looked over the styles on the previous page one style probably struck you as being totally opposite of the way you approach life. That's the one you rated as number four. That's your villain role.

After you have circled your three roles, answer the questions at the bottom of the page regarding the advantages and disadvantages of your style. After you finish, find a time to meet with your co-captain(s). If you're the only captain for the season, simply skip that page.

It's vital to have a strong connection with all team captains. You'll gain a better understanding of the team leaders by understanding each other's style. Have a discussion with all team captains and cover everyone's leading roles, supporting roles, and villain roles.

Then discuss the differences you see. You'll need to be aware of these throughout the season. The last question is the most important. What's the plan to work through these differences?

Your Leadership Style

Your Leading Role—Circle the role that best describes how you lead based on the information within this chapter.

Togetherness   Enterpriser   Analyzer   Motivator

Your Supporting Role—Circle the role that best describes the second way you may lead based on the information within this chapter.

Togetherness   Enterpriser   Analyzer   Motivator

Your Villain Role—Circle the role that least explains the way you lead based on the information within this chapter. (This would be the one type that you're sure doesn't fit you.)

Togetherness   Enterpriser   Analyzer   Motivator

As a team captain, what are the advantages of your leading role?

What are the disadvantages of your leading role?

Your Co-Captain's Leadership Style

Your Co-Captain's Leading Role—Circle the role that best describes how your co-captain leads based on the information within this chapter.

Togetherness   Enterpriser   Analyzer   Motivator

Your Co-Captain's Supporting Role—Circle the role that best describes the second way your co-captain may lead based on the information within this chapter.

Togetherness   Enterpriser   Analyzer   Motivator

Your Co-Captain's Villain Role—Circle the role that least describes the way your co-captain leads based on the information within this chapter. (This would be the one type that your co-captain says doesn't fit at all.)

Togetherness   Enterpriser   Analyzer   Motivator

As you evaluate your co-captain's leading role, what are the similarities you share?

What potential differences could arise this season based on your styles?

How will you and your co-captain work through those differences?

Embracing Your Leadership Style

People often ask me which style is the best for being a team captain. The answer is simple. There isn't one. Don't fall into the trap of thinking one style is better than another style. Each style brings strengths and weaknesses to the team. The key is to understand your style and then figure out the best way to help the team.

During the season, each style will deal with situations differently. Great captains understand this and may call upon different people at different times to handle different situations. Differences in people don't equal bad, difference equals difference.

"

Leadership Style

"You have no control over what the other person does. You only have control over what you do."

—A. J. Kitt

"A successful team beats with one heart."

—Sara Redmond

"Just as in a stained-glass window—if there was only one color it would not be beautiful. On our team—if there was only one player, it would not be victorious."

—Unknown

"

CAPTAIN'S CLIPBOARD

Four Leadership Styles

Differences in leadership styles between you, your co-captain, and your coaches can make your team stronger or weaker. You get to choose. Be flexible enough to alter your leadership style according to each situation that arises.

Togetherness

Enterpriser

Analyzer

Motivator

PART 2

GET
SET

CHAPTER 4
Creating Team Chemistry

Great chemists understand that when elements are combined, something greater than the individual parts can be created. Combine gas with a spark, you create a fire. Mix hydrogen with oxygen, you get water. Combine baking soda with vinegar, and you have a miniature volcano.

When the elements are combined, they make something they couldn't have created if they had stayed in their original form.

The same philosophy applies to great teamwork. As individuals you're limited. But when you come together and form a team, you will be able to create something significant.

Before gasoline engines were invented, farmers would take their strongest horse and see how much weight it could pull on a wagon. This is similar to what we have today with truck and tractor pulls. At one county fair, the first-place horse pulled 1,000 pounds, and the second-place horse pulled 850 pounds. The farmers began to wonder how much the two horses could pull together. Logic would say 1,850 pounds. Yet when the horses were put together, they pulled 2,500 pounds. It was the combination of the two that allowed them to pull that much weight.

If you're going to have a season of significance and play beyond the scoreboard, you won't be able to do it by yourself. Some of you are involved in a sport where you have to rely on a strong team to achieve success. Others of you participate in sports that are individually oriented. Even with sports such as gymnastics, track, wrestling, and tennis, the individual scores, matches, and points are added up at the end of each competition to create a team score. No matter the sport, team chemistry is vital.

It's fascinating listening to coaches being interviewed after the season. If the season was disappointing, you'll hear something like, "the chemistry just wasn't there." Contrast that with a season of significance where coaches say, "Our team chemistry was tremendous."

Combining a bunch of talented individuals doesn't create a great team. It creates a bunch of individuals who are on a team. Most coaches would rather coach a team with average talent and strong chemistry than a bunch of highly talented individuals who are only concerned about individual accomplishments.

Team chemistry boils down to seven elements. Combine these elements, and you are on your way to a season of significance. Team captains have to be master chemists. They must look at the team and decide how much of each element to add for a season of significance. This chapter gives you an overview of creating team chemistry. You may have a great deal of influence on some of the elements while you'll have less influence on some of the others. The key is to work on the elements you can improve.

The seven elements are:

- Camaraderie
- Confidence
- Communication
- Commitment
- Coachable
- Consistency
- Character

Element # 1: Camaraderie

Here's the first question to ask: Is the sport fun? When I ask students why they participate in athletics, the number one thing that they say is, "It's fun." Most teens tell me if it's not fun, they don't want to be involved.

Now, is it always going to be fun? Of course not. There are several things you have to go through that are not a lot of fun. The first two weeks of conditioning are not fun. Having teammates complain about everything under the sun is not fun. Practicing in extreme conditions is not fun. However, you should be enjoying your sport at least 80% of the time.

To increase the fun factor of your sport, look for ways teammates can get to know each other and enjoy being with each other. Creating fun events and traditions on and off the court can develop camaraderie. Our high school football team had one tradition that is still with me today. It was called "the pit." We played in an old stone stadium that was built in the 1940s. There was a small room built into the stadium with a dirt floor that stored track and football equipment. It had a musty smell because of little air circulation. When the door was shut, it was pitch dark.

Every Thursday after practice, our entire team would pile into the pit. After everyone was in, the head coach would walk in and shut the door behind him. No one could see a thing, and the only thing you could hear was breathing. After five minutes of complete silence, the coach would tell a motivational story. After his story, he opened the floor up to the team captains and then to any person in the room to say whatever was on their heart. The code was, "whatever is said in the pit, stays in the pit."

I can't tell you specifics of what was said, but I can tell you that guys poured their hearts out. They said how much it meant to them to be a part of this team. They complimented the work ethic of specific individuals. Some teammates had powerful stories of their own to share. Throughout the week, we looked forward to Thursday's practice because we knew we were going into the pit.

Whenever I speak of or write about "the pit," I get goose bumps. When our class gets together for reunions, we spend at least an hour talking about the power of the pit. Years later, it is still with each member of the team.

So what will your team do this year to create camaraderie? Can you implement fun contests at the end of practice? Is there a drill or song you can do or sing after practice? Could you do an activity or play a different sport for fifteen minutes? Maybe a quick game of kickball is in order. How about showing up to cheer for another team from your school? By showing up for other people's games, you're creating camaraderie with your team while also creating school spirit. When this happens, other teams will often do the same for you.

Team chemistry incorporates camaraderie. Make sure you're having fun and planning fun events for the team.

Element # 2: Confidence

There is a thin line between confidence and arrogance. While the line is thin, the results are not. Confidence is the feeling that you have a good chance of winning. Arrogance is the belief that you can't be beat.

When I ask students what they would like to work on in a leadership training, several usually choose the topic of confidence. While I can't *give* you confidence, I can tell you how to *get* confidence. There are four steps to gaining confidence as an individual and as a team.

- **Step #1: Recognize that you're afraid to look like a fool.** If you've ever driven a car with a manual transmission, you know what I'm talking about. You shift from one gear to the next while pushing in the clutch with no effort or thought. Most people think, "It looks easy, but there's no way I'm trying that. I'd look like an idiot if I tried."

It's the fear of looking bad that holds most of us back from reaching our true potential. Sometimes, we don't even try because of our fears.

Then someone encourages you to give it a try. That someone usually remembers what it was like to learn. Maybe she says, "Oh, you'll probably kill the engine. Sometimes, you'll feel like you're riding a wild horse, but that happened to me. You'll get the hang of it after you try it a few times."

As soon as you get into the driver's seat, you're overcoming your fear and preparing for step two. As soon as you let out the clutch the first time, you're on to step two.

- **Step #2: Look like a fool.** When you let the clutch out, the car shook wildly and probably stopped. Then your friend or parent gave you a dicey stare, and you gave it another try. Ten minutes later, you were out of the driveway and onto the street. You still probably looked a little foolish, but at least you were going from first gear to second instead of from first to fourth. Now you're at step three.

- **Step #3: Be on the verge.** This step feels uncomfortable because you're totally concentrating on what you're doing and sometimes it's working and sometimes it's not. It's like concentrating on letting out the clutch as you find the right gear. After several hours or days of practice with a capable teacher, you're approaching step four.

- **Step #4: Master the skill confidently.** When you reach this step, you feel comfortable with what you've learned and you no longer have to consciously think about what you're doing. It now comes naturally. As you're driving that car with manual transmission, you can listen to the radio and talk with a friend while shifting from one gear to the next. Confidence is an awesome feeling.

After you master one skill, you must go through the same four steps the next time to learn something new. You go back to the beginning, which doesn't feel good. But that's how you make progress. Whether it's driving a car with a manual transmission or learning a new set of plays, you will go through all four steps. Get through step one and two as fast as you can so you can excel your progress.

How do you get confidence? Experience. How do you get experience? By messing up, learning something important, and then applying the wisdom you gained in the next situation.

Element #3: Communication

Examples of effective communication include people constantly making valuable comments, teammates talking to each other on and off the court of competition, and asking questions when instructions are not clear. It's impossible to read someone's mind. Thoughts and ideas must be communicated clearly.

There are five tips on communication that will create a close-knit team.

Tip #1: Think before you speak. How many times have you said something and then wished you could take it back? I was in a training program in Salt Lake City when a participant asked a female when she was going to have the baby. Her face immediately turned red and she said, "I'm not pregnant, I'm just fat." Needless to say, the rest of the day was a disaster for the person who didn't think before he asked the question.

You don't have to think about every word, but take a second to think about the best way to say what you want to say. For example, if you said to someone who appears to be having a bad day, "What's your problem?" he probably wouldn't respond. However, if you walked up to him and asked, "You don't seem like yourself, what's up?" he would probably open up to you and share what's going through his mind. It's the same situation, but a different approach encourages a different response.

Tip #2: Criticize with care. Have you ever seen magicians pierce a balloon with a long needle? They get the point of the needle through while keeping the balloon intact. The same principle works with criticism. No one likes to be criticized. There are times when you or a coach has to do it. The key is to get the point through and still leave the individual or team intact.

There is an exception, of course. There are

times when a team needs a serious shake up. Sometimes the only way to do that is to raise your voice and really lay it on the line. If the practice stunk or teammates were not mentally showing up for a game, it may be time to shake things up.

But here's the distinction. You can "lose your cool" only two or three times in a season. If coaches or captains resort to yelling and screaming on a consistent basis, that type of communication will lose its effect. If you've ever been around a coach or captain who rips into a team every day, you learn to tune out the volume so that it doesn't even bother or affect you any more.

Tip #3: Use people's names. Even if you're from a school with thousands of students and your team has a lot of members, make sure everyone knows all the names. People love hearing their name called.

Great team leaders even get the officials' names during the opening rules and address each official by name. When you use people's names, you become a top-notch individual and team.

Tip #4: Use sign language. Actions also speak loudly. Give a nod of confidence to a teammate who appears nervous. Pat a teammate on the back after she messes up. Look at the basket to show that you're open for a pass to slam-dunk the basketball.

In the heat of competition, you may not be able to verbally tell someone what you're thinking. A quick sign is all that you need. Develop and discuss some signs during a practice or team meeting. Other signs are just driven by gut instinct; they cannot be practiced at all.

Tip #5: Ask questions. If you don't understand what the coach is saying, ask for clarification. Great teams have open communication with the coaching staff. Avoid acting on instructions when you don't have a true understanding of what you're supposed to do.

When you ask, have a tone of voice that will create a positive response. Listen to the answer and then implement the idea.

Element #4: Commitment

Commitment is demonstrated during the season and in the off season. Despite what some people say, I believe high school athletes do not have to dedicate themselves to their sports year round. I believe you should have all kinds of interests as you go through high school. If you train year round for a single sport, you will miss out on some great aspects of high school. With that said, there are some things you can do during the off season to increase the odds of a season of significance.

Spend some time with your team-mates. As a team captain, schedule informal practices during the off season. Consider taking part in a summer league that keeps you in shape. Most athletes would benefit from spending some time in the weight room. Being in shape never hurts anyone. When you're in shape, you feel better about yourself, have more energy, and you can deal with stress easier.

Spending time with your teammates creates chemistry that will be valuable when the season begins. There is an important distinction to make regarding time together and relationships. *Great teams recognize you don't have to be best friends with everyone on the team to have a season of significance.* There will be many times when you have someone on the team you may either feel neutral about or don't care for. The best teams can leave it at the door. They know when it's time to practice or play, it's show time. Top-notch teams have the ability to play together even when they're not best friends. The key is to accept people where they are and perform the best you can as a team.

Element # 5: Coachable

Do your teammates listen to the coach and then do as they're told? Can teammates deal with constructive feedback? Do people mentally shut down if they're asked to change their attitude or actions?

Teams and individuals that are coachable look for ways to improve. The top athletes in the world all have a coach. Why? Because they can't see what they're doing right and what they're doing wrong because they're in the middle of the action.

Have you ever seen yourself on video and thought, "That's how I look? I thought I looked better than that." Have you ever heard your own voice on a recording and thought it was someone else? That was you, and that's exactly how you looked and sounded, whether you liked it or not.

In one of my workshops I teach the skill of juggling. Most people don't know how to juggle, and they doubt I can teach it to them. Yet within ninety minutes or less, I can teach 85% of the people in my audience.

Before I start, we discuss what holds people back from learning or being coached. Responses include: bad attitude, fear of rejection, fear of failure, poor instruction, past performance, no motivation, being stubborn, having a large ego, not listening to instructions, and lack of incentive. I then challenge the students to suspend those thoughts or habits and completely immerse themselves into the juggling activity and be 100% coachable.

After they accept that challenge, they seek a feedback buddy. The role of the feedback buddy is to give observations, encouragement, and instructions to the person who is learning how to juggle. After one person masters a component of juggling, the roles are reversed.

A great feedback buddy will tell his partner what he sees the partner doing right and what the partner can improve on. A poor feedback buddy watches his partner not following instructions and lets it go without giving his partner the information to correct the problem. A poor feedback buddy becomes indifferent to his partner's progress.

As a team, you must be willing to be coachable. When you hear an idea that could improve your performance, give it a try even if it feels uncomfortable. Remember: Others can see what we can't.

Establish feedback buddies on the team. When the time is right, give feedback on what you saw worked well and maybe an idea or two for your buddy to try the next time a similar situation appears. The team's growth will be incredible to watch. No matter how great a team is or how great the players *think* they are, there is always room for improvement. As Robby Naish says, "Strive to be the best you can be.... Focus, watch, listen, and learn. Try to never be satisfied with good enough...and above all, love what you do."

Element # 6: Consistency

It's interesting to watch teams perform from one contest to another. Some teams perform at consistent levels. Others will defeat a state-ranked team one week and then lose to a team that hasn't won all year the following week.

Effective teams play at a consistent level and pace. They know how to turn their efforts up a notch when necessary, but they don't rely on having to produce an outstanding performance

every game. Playing at a high level leads to burn out in a hurry. It's important to understand the appropriate pace.

What does a pace car do at the races? It keeps the pack together and then gets them up to the speed to race. If teams stay together and set a strong pace with their work ethic and attitude, they can avoid the big letdowns during the season.

As a team leader, you're the pace car. When your teammates are sulking from a resent loss, the odds of having a season of significance are low. When this happens, be the voice that brings them up—even if you feel just like they do. Great teams and team leaders work hard on being positive even when they don't want to be.

Have you ever walked into practice when you didn't have the energy to be there? After you got started, your body was in motion and suddenly you forgot you didn't want to be there. *The motion created the emotion.* Your energy level increased, and you had a strong practice. Too many teams play and practice great only when they *feel* like it.

Top-notch teams play and practice hard whether they feel like it or not. They understand it takes motion to create the emotion. It's important to understand how to manage your energy throughout the season.

There are two energy gears: positive low and positive high. Teams must know what gear they have to use in order to attain their desired goal. The positive-low gear is upbeat, alert, and ready to go. The positive-high energy gear is the feeling of going all out, not holding back, and that there is no tomorrow.

Each gear must be used at a different time. Maybe you're in the middle of the season. The positive-low gear may be appropriate for team meetings and practices. However, there are times when the positive-low gear is not enough, such as during a game against a key rival or preparing for a tournament. You and the coaching staff must gauge the appropriate pace to use at various times during the game and during the season. If you have back-to-back games on the same day, and you win the first one and waste a bunch of energy celebrating, watch out for game two. If too much energy was spent celebrating, performing well in the second game is going to be difficult.

For each situation, think about which gear to use. There will be times when you need to quickly go from a positive-low gear to a positive-high gear and then back to the positive-low gear. The best teams understand how and when to do that.

Element #7: Character

Great teams never count themselves out no matter how remote the chances of victory are. They compete every second of every game. Giving in is not an option.

As a Minnesota Twins fan, I still remember the 1991 season. The Twins had lost game five in Atlanta during the World Series and were returning to the Metrodome down three games to two. In order to be world champions, they needed to win the final two games.

Kirby Puckett of the Minnesota Twins had a below-average performance in game five. Before game six, he told his team-mates, "Don't worry about it guys, just ride on my back tonight." That night, Kirby hit the game winning home run that sent the series into game seven. The Twins went on to win game seven and become world champions. They won the World Series because the team had character. Does your team have character?

Teams with character trust each other. They know they can rely on each other to go all out no matter what the scoreboard says. They have an inner drive to work hard and play hard. They can bounce back from a loss or a disappointing season. They don't crumble when someone gets injured and is out for the rest of the season.

Teams with character look adversity in the eye and smile because they will not be denied a season of significance. In 2000, the U.S. women's soccer team had to overcome the odds of injuries and people's doubts during the Olympic games. But in the end, they captured the gold. The celebration after the final second ticked off the scoreboard will be etched in the minds of millions of Americans who were watching the game. The team's character defined their destination.

The same thing will be true for your team. If you have developed character, you will have a season of significance regardless of your team's record. Many teams are remembered not because they had a winning record, but because they were a group of athletes who acted with character and simply did the best they could with the talent they had.

A Strong Team

So when you're trying to build a strong team, remember the seven C's of team chemistry: camaraderie, confidence, communication, commitment, coachable, consistency, and character. When these seven elements come together, you'll create a season of significance.

In his book, *The Winner Within*, Pat Riley hits the nail on the head when he describes teamwork. He says, "My driving belief is this: great teamwork is the only way to reach our ulti-mate moments, to create breakthroughs that define our careers, to fulfill our lives with a sense of lasting significance."

He then says, "Our best efforts, combined with those of our teammates, grow into something far greater and far more sat-isfying than anything we could have achieved on our own. Teams make us part of something that matters. They are the fountain from which all our rewards will ultimately flow."

Teamwork

"Even when you've played the game of your life, it's the feeling of teamwork that you'll remember. You'll forget the plays, the shots, and the scores, but you'll never forget your teammates."

—Deborah Palmore

"No matter how much I've won, or how much outside praise has come my way, or where it goes from here, there's one clear fact that has never, ever been lost on me. I didn't do this alone."

—Power Bar

"It's important to respect both your team-mates and your opponents. Friendships can make a victory last forever."

—Kamie Koven

"

"You play for the name on the front, not the name on the back."

—Duane Sutter

"Sports can unite a group of people from different backgrounds, all working together to achieve a common goal. Even if they fall short, sharing that journey is an experience they'll never forget."

—Ahmad Rashad

"Teamwork is the fuel that allows common people to produce uncommon results."

—Unknown

"It's easy to figure out who isn't a team player. They'll constantly remind the coach just how good they are."

—Brian Jett

continued…

"

"

"Teammates are there for each other even after the noise of the crowd is gone."

—Jim Brown

"The way a team plays as a whole determines it's success. You may have the greatest bunch of individual stars in the world, but if they don't play together, the club won't be worth a dime."

—Babe Ruth

"It's what you learn after you know it all that counts."

—John Wooden

"

CAPTAIN'S CLIPBOARD

Seven Elements of Team Chemistry

1. Camaraderie

2. Confidence

3. Communication

4. Commitment

5. Coachable

6. Consistency

7. Character

CHAPTER 5

Creating a Team Vision

If you don't know where you're headed, your team is going to struggle. It's like someone jumping into a taxicab without a destination in mind. Imagine the cost of the ride if someone said to the cab driver, "Just drive around for awhile, and when I see the right place, I'll tell you." What a costly approach.

Great teams can see their destination. They see the big picture.

During the grand opening of Disney World in Orlando, Florida, there was a huge celebration. Unfortunately, Walt Disney had passed away prior to the doors opening to the public. After the ceremony, the emcee of the event said to Walt's wife, "It's too bad Walt wasn't here to see it." Mrs. Disney turned to the emcee and said, "Oh, he saw every bit of it in his mind."

Walt Disney saw the big picture. Does your team see the big picture?

If the big picture isn't defined clearly and communicated often, your teammates will begin a chain of complaining. They will complain about physical conditioning, watching films, and the amount of playing time they get.

A strong team vision can decrease this complaining. It won't eliminate it, but it will keep the complaining down. Strong captains do everything in their power to keep complaining to a minimum, and they know that they won't be able to completely eliminate it because there will always be some complaining.

To create a strong vision for the season, follow the GOALS formula, which I developed. The GOALS formula has helped thousands of individuals and hundreds of teams reach a desired outcome. Just like exercise equipment, it only works when you use it. If you follow the system, you will see results.

The GOALS formula stands for:

- **G**enuine

- **O**ptimistic

- **A**ccurate

- **L**isted Out

- **S**ymbols

Genuine

Have you ever had someone else set a goal for you? When that happened, were you excited about accomplishing it? Usually, the answer is no. You're not pumped about it, because it's not your goal. It's someone else's vision for you.

Remember when you were a child, and you really wanted a new toy that was advertised on TV? Maybe you didn't have the money, and your parents said they wouldn't pay for it. What did you do? If you really wanted it, which is what a genuine desire is, you got creative and started earning some money. Remember the pride and satisfaction of going to the store with a plastic bag full of change and saying, "I've got just enough." You worked hard because it was your goal—not someone else's.

So what do you want to accomplish this season? What could the team achieve this season? Use the surveys and goal sheets in chapter six to help you set goals as a team. If you have a genuine desire to achieve, you are well on your way.

Optimistic

There are four approaches to setting goals: Pessimistic, realistic, optimistic and idealistic. Pessimistic goals are for people who expect little from themselves and their team. Realistic goals are for people who expect average results from themselves and others. Idealistic goals are so high in the sky they're impossible to achieve. Optimistic goals are out of your reach, but they're not out of your sight. You want to set optimistic goals.

As you define goals for yourself and your team, ask yourself this question: Is the goal going to be a stretch or will it be sim-

ple to reach? If it's not going to take much effort to accomplish the goal, it won't mean much when you attain it. I'm challenging you to set optimistic goals for yourself and your team. If you're wondering if you can reach that far, you're setting optimistic goals.

Accurate

As I walk into schools for a leadership training or school assembly in the fall, I usually meet with a small group of students to get a flavor for school spirit, attitudes, and culture. After visiting for a few minutes, I ask students, "What is your goal for this school year?" Most look at me like a deer caught in headlights. Typically, I see students shrug their shoulders and sheepishly say, "I don't know, graduate on time I guess."

Talk about a vague, unclear vision of the future! Every once in a while, I'll hear, "My goal is to graduate with a 3.5 GPA, be selected all conference in _____ (name of the sport), and get accepted into _____ (name of college)."

After a response like that, I smile, and say, "It sounds like you have an accurate view of the future."

Is your goal accurate or vague?

You'll have a stronger chance of attaining your goal if it's precise in nature. For example, a team may set a goal regarding the average number of goals scored in a game. Most teams set several goals in several areas. Individuals should also be setting goals for the season. Remember, set team goals first, then set individual goals.

Listed Out

Have you ever invited a group of friends for a sleep over? Suddenly it's 3:00 am and despite the fact you've eaten three pizzas and downed a case of soda, everyone's still hungry. So you tiptoe into the kitchen so you won't wake your parents and find a cake mix. Everyone's in agreement: It's cake time. You empty the box and start adding the ingredients. Then you realize you don't have any of the ingredients required. Someone gets the smart idea to just add water and see what happens. Because you're all starving, you crank the temperature to 550 degrees and put the cake mix in. After ten minutes, you discover the cake has exploded all over the inside of the oven. What happened?

You didn't follow the recipe.

A recipe is basically a list of ingredients and the sequence for adding them in order to get the results you desire. If you're going to reach your optimistic goal, you must create a list that shows how you're going to achieve your goal. If your goal is to serve three aces in volleyball, you have to create a list of what you need to do to improve your serve. The list must be accurate and measurable. If you write, "Try harder or practice more," you're creating a vague list. However, if you created a list that included these items, you're on your way.

- Watch an instructional video on killer serves.

- Hit thirty extra serves after practice every night.

- Increase strength by doing forty-five push-ups every morning right after getting out of bed.

Specific actions will lead you to your goal. Great recipes, just like great goals, have a list that outlines specifically how they will be attained.

Symbols

Your mind is powerful. Just think about what it does. Have you ever had a dream in which you were falling, and you woke up to find your heart racing? Have you been swimming in a lake and had to get out because the music from the movie *Jaws* starts playing in your mind? Have you ever heard a song and immediately remembered a person or a situation? Have you ever forgot to set your alarm but woke up at the time you were going to set it for?

If you have experienced any of these situations, you've had a glimpse of the power of your mind. Great teams understand the power of the mind and then harness it to help them reach their goals.

Create symbols that will help direct your mind and the mind of your teammates toward a certain goal. For example, if your team's goal is to make it to the state playoffs, find pictures of where the event will take place and post them in the locker room.

Seeing symbols puts the mind to work. Symbols can create a sense of confidence in the mind that says, "This is going to happen." When people see these symbols, they start to believe it. Even if you fall short, at least you had the courage to aim your efforts high.

Reaching Your Goals

Obtaining your goals boils down to commitment. If your team-mates are truly committed to each other and to a common goal, you have an excellent chance of attaining it. Great teams know where they're going this season. They take the time and effort to fill out the personal and team goals in chapter six. They present the big picture to the team and keep talking about it. You've got to see it to be it!

Vision and Goals

"I learned how to visualize. If I have a match the next day, I visualize serving the ball and playing the game—and winning. So, when I actually play the match, I've already done it in my mind, fifty times."

—Beatriz "Gigi" Fernandez

"There are three types of baseball players—those who make it happen, those who watch it happen, and those who wonder what happened."

—Tommy Lasorda

"It's fun to set goals, reach goals, and reset them."

—Bonnie Blair

"I always had something to shoot for each year: to jump one inch further."

—Jackie Joyner-Kersee

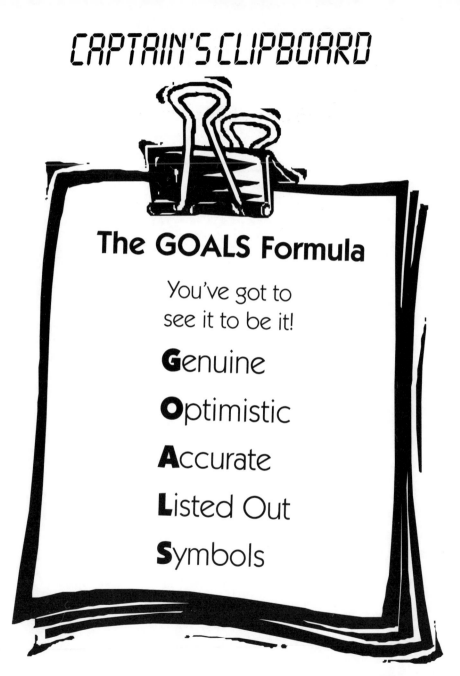

CAPTAIN'S CLIPBOARD

The GOALS Formula

You've got to
see it to be it!

Genuine

Optimistic

Accurate

Listed Out

Symbols

CHAPTER 6
Preseason Preparations

A season of significance doesn't just happen. It must be carefully planned. It's best to start planning a few months before the season begins. If planning starts the day before everyone shows up for the first practice, it's going to be difficult to create the kind of team climate necessary for a season of significance.

You may be thinking, "That seems like a lot of thinking and a lot of work." It's tempting just to fly by the seat of your pants and deal with the issues as they come up. That's the approach of average captains. If you've read this far in the book, it's obvious you aren't interested in being an average leader.

To plan well and lay the groundwork for a great season, complete the questions and exercises in this chapter. Take a few moments and fill out the preseason questionnaires. The first three you can do alone. The last two surveys are to be completed with your head coach. If you are committed to being a captain, take the time to fill them all out.

Preseason
Team
Questionnaire

Chapter five on creating a team vision emphasized the importance of a common goal. This survey will help you see the big
picture for the upcoming season.

- **Theme for the season** — Great teams define the season
  through a theme. In my work with hundreds of teams
  since 1990, I've seen a number of creative themes.
  Examples of themes could include: "It's our time," "All out
  all the time," "Don't set your goals to your ability, set your
  ability to your goals," or "United we stand, divided we
  fall." Consider printing your theme on a banner and place
  it in your locker room as a constant reminder to everyone
  who enters.

- **Theme song** — Is there a hot new song that reflects the
  team's makeup? Get the song and play it before games.
  Music can rapidly change our moods. Make sure the song
  doesn't have any questionable lyrics. When the song is
  played years from now, all the team members will think
  back to the year it was used as your team's theme song.

- **T-Shirt design** — Having a T-shirt printed for each team
  member can create unity. Team members could wear
  these T-shirts on the day of a game or a match. When your
  classmates see the team wearing these T-shirts in the hall-
  way between classes, they will be reminded to attend
  your game.

- **Team strengths** — What are the team's strongest assets?
  Will several people from last year's team be returning? Do

the players have a strong work ethic? Is the coach implementing a new system? These are items to use as building blocks for a significant season.

• **Team concerns** — Now think about your team's weaknesses. What is going to be difficult to work with this year? Do people have poor attitudes? Are your teammates lacking motivation? Is there a lack of talent? This will be important since you may be able to do something during the off season to improve on the weaknesses.

• **Objective goals** — Objective goals are measurable. Examples include: your record (your wins and losses), average points scored each game, number of aces served, and other measurable statistics. At the end of the season, you would be able to see if these were attained by examining the statistics from the season.

• **Subjective goals** — These goals are difficult to measure. They may include: creating a feeling that everyone contributed to the team, having fun throughout the season, and demonstrating strong sportsmanship. No statistic book would be able to measure these goals. However, they are important.

• **How will this team be remembered?** How will your team go down in history? Will you be remembered as a group of people who worked very hard or a team that didn't have much talent but made the most of it? Hopefully, your team won't be remembered as a bunch of individuals who could care less about each other and didn't perform to their potential. Think about the answers to these questions before the season starts.

Preseason Team Questionnaire

Theme for the Season

Theme Song

T-Shirt Design

Team Strength

Team Concerns

Objective Goals

Subjective Goals

How Will This Team Be Remembered?

Preseason Personal Leadership Questionnaire

This preseason personal leadership survey is designed to help you take a closer look at your leadership ability. It's a questionnaire about being a captain and what your strengths and weaknesses are.

- **Leadership strengths** — What skills or attributes have you gained or experienced that will make you a great leader? Are you good with people? Can you listen effectively? Are you easy to approach?

- **Areas of concern** — What scares you about being a captain this year? Some captains are concerned about filling the shoes from the previous year's captains. Others are concerned about making decisions that affect the team. Identify the concerns and write them down so you can begin to address them as the season approaches.

- **Areas of improvement** — Which area or weakness could you address prior to the season? What do you need to learn about dealing with conflict? Is your work ethic as strong as it could be? Do you make negative comments to teammates? All captains have an area they can improve on.

- **Your off-season preparations** — What have you done to mentally prepare for the role of captain? Did you attend a leadership camp? Have you read a great book on teen leadership? (Additional leadership resources are listed in the back of this book. See Appendix 1: Resources.)

Have you spent time getting to know your teammates in the off-season?

- **Your legacy** — The bottom line question to ask yourself is this: *As a team leader, I will be remembered as a person who. . . ?* When the season is finished, what will others remember about the season and you as a captain? What will they say at your ten-year high school reunion? Will you be remembered as someone who really cared about the team? Will teammates describe you as a captain who inspired others to go beyond their best? Too often team captains are remembered for their lack of motivation or letting the role go to their head. By answering this question, you will start to create your mental approach. Keep in mind, your team will be remembered. The question is *how* will it be remembered?

Preseason
Personal Leadership
Questionnaire

Leadership Strengths

Areas of Concern

Areas of Improvement

Off-Season Preparations

How Will I Be Remembered as a Team Leader?

Preseason Personal Ability Questionnaire

This survey will examine your skill level in your activity or sport. It will help you identify how you can prepare for the season while emphasizing your strengths and working on your weaknesses.

- **Strengths** — What skills have you mastered in your given sport? Is your floor routine incredible? Does your overhand serve leave your opponent in awe? Can you shoot a three-point shot from anywhere on the court? These skills will serve as a foundation for the season.

- **Areas of concern** — Do you have an injury that has held you back? Are you going to be in a new position this year? Are you in good physical shape?

- **Areas of improvement** — What areas still need some work? Do you need to increase your flexibility so your high kicks can be higher for the new dance line? Did you scratch too often in the long jump last year? Once these issues are addressed, you will be able to tackle the steps needed to improve them.

- **Off-season preparations** — Did you attend a camp that specializes in your sport? Were you involved in a summer league? Did you watch an instructional video that gave additional insight?

- **Objective goals** — These are measurable goals you are aiming your sights at. They could include: average number of aces in a match, the total number of yards gained in a season, or the batting average for the year. They could also include post-season awards such as all-conference. These should be specific goals that can be measured by a statistic book.

- **Subjective goals** — These are difficult to measure, but important to make. Examples include: working hard every practice, supporting teammates, respecting officials' calls, or being a good sport regardless of the game's outcome.

- **Your legacy** — In evaluating your level of play, ask yourself this question: *As a player what will I be remembered for?* How will I leave my mark this season? Will I be someone with talent and class? A person who puts the team first and statistics last?

These questionnaires can appear to be a pain to complete. It would be easier just to glance at them and not fill them out. However, by taking the time to go through it now you are creating a working plan for the season.

Preseason
Personal Ability Questionnaire

Strengths

Areas of Concern

Areas of Improvement

Off-Season Preparations

Objective Goals

Subjective Goals

How Will I Be Remembered as a Player?

Coach to Captain Questionnaire

This final survey pertains to your coach. Give the "Coach to Captain Questionnaire" to your coach and ask him to answer the questions before the two of you meet. If your coach doesn't have time, set up a time to meet and fill it in together. It's imperative to have this discussion prior to the first practice or sometime during your preseason. Your coach's responses will create an interesting conversation as you compare thoughts regarding the season ahead.

The results of this survey will prove to be valuable throughout the season. It's designed to shed some light on several topics that are often not discussed. It will create a code of conduct for both the captain and the coach.

- **Expectations** — Ask: *What do you expect from me this season?* Frustrations occur when one person has unmet expectations with another person. Too often, these expectations have never been communicated. Your goal is to get a clear definition of your role as a captain this season. Try to get a clear definition of what your coach wants from you.

- **Job description** — Ask: *If you were to write a job description for me this season, what would it say?* Chances are this is your first experience as a team captain. You are looking for specific responses in this question. A job description should include a description of what the coach expects from you every day as well as a description of what's expected of you for the overall season.

- **Your contribution to your coach** — Ask: *How can I help you this season?* This question might blow your coach away. Usually, captains focus on what can the coach do for them. Coaching is a difficult job. This question is designed to show your coach you want the season to be significant and that you're thinking of the team instead of just yourself.

- **Process for grievances** — Ask: *What's the process to address problems or concerns this season?* Every team has to deal with issues during the season. When these issues pop their ugly heads, it's key to have a plan of attack. Average teams just let things slide and hope these difficulties go away. Teams who play beyond the scoreboard face each problem and deal with it appropriately.

  Assume a player has a problem or concern with the coach. Some coaches ask the captain to bring the concern to the coach at a meeting. Other coaches encourage the captain to ask the player to approach the coach directly. The key to is to *define* the process. As a captain, you must know the process that you and your coach will commit to work through the difficult times.

- **Other information** — Ask: *What do I need to understand that I may not?* This will create an interesting response from your coach. The response may be simple or complex. It will certainly provide a piece of information your wouldn't have gathered without asking the question. Keep in mind, if your coach gives feedback for personal areas of improvement, a strong team captain will listen and absorb the information without becoming heated or defensive.

- **Your coach's leading style** — Ask your coach which leading style he falls into. Chapter three outlines four different leadership styles. Have your coach review these styles. Ask which style is your coach's leading role, supporting role, and villain role. This will prove to be valuable information as you continue to communicate with your coach throughout the season.

Coach to Captain Questionnaire

What do you expect from me personally this season?

If you were to write a job description for me this season, what would it look like?

How can I help you this season?

What's the process to address problems and concerns this season?

What do I need to understand that I may not know?

What's your leading style? (Circle one. See chapter three for a description of each style.)

    Togetherness   Enterpriser   Analyzer   Motivator

What's your supporting style? (Circle one.)

    Togetherness   Enterpriser   Analyzer   Motivator

What's your villain style? (Circle one.)

    Togetherness   Enterpriser   Analyzer   Motivator

Coach's Vision Questionnaire

Another valuable questionnaire is the "The Coach's Vision Questionnaire." Ask your coach to fill out this survey or set up a meeting to talk about these questions. These are the same questions that appeared in the "Preseason Personal Ability Questionnaire" that you filled out earlier. What's good about having your coach complete this survey is that it gives you another perspective—your coach's. The more feedback you have, the better.

The Coach's Vision Questionnaire

Strengths

Areas of Concern

Areas of Improvement

Off-Season Preparations

Objective Goals

Subjective Goals

This page left intentionally blank

Preparation

"It's not the will to win that matters—every-one has that. It's the will to prepare to win that matters."

—Paul "Bear" Bryant

"Win or lose, you will never regret working hard, making sacrifices, being disciplined, or focusing too much. Success is measured by what we have done to prepare for the com-petition."

—John Smith

"The glory of sport comes from dedication, determination, and desire. Achieving suc-cess and personal glory in athletics has less to do with wins and losses than it does with learning how to prepare yourself so that at the end of the day, whether on the track or in the office, you know that there was noth-ing more you could have done to reach your ultimate goal."

—Jackie Joyner-Kersee

CAPTAIN'S CLIPBOARD

Preparation for the Preseason

Failing to prepare, is preparing to fail. As you complete each preseason questionnaire, check them off:

- Preseason Team Questionnaire

- Preseason Personal Leadership Questionnaire

- Preseason Personal Ability Questionnaire

- Coach to Captain Questionnaire

- The Coach's Vision Questionnaire

CHAPTER 7
The Delusion of Drugs

Imagine a smooth voice on a television advertisement asking, "Are you looking for a way to destroy your health, lose friends, and slow your team's progress?" Who would say yes to this product?

No one!

Yet every year teen athletes say yes to illegal drugs, alcohol, and performance-enhancing drugs.

Before you skip this chapter because another adult is telling you to "just say no," read the information and think about how drugs affect your team—even if you are not the one taking them.

What If?

A football team in northern Minnesota won a regional final and were set to play for the state championship at the Metrodome in Minneapolis where the Minnesota Vikings and the Minnesota Twins play. After the regional victory, the team had a party where alcohol was served. On their way home, two all-conference linemen were pulled over by the police and cited for minor consumption. Because of their infraction, they became ineligible for the state championship.

The team lost in the finals. If the two linemen participated, would the team have won the state championship? No one can answer that question for sure, but everyone will remember that question for a long time. Imagine their ten-year reunion when everyone gathers to share old memories. The conversation among the football team will surely discuss what could have been.

Imagine the two former linemen show-ing up for the reunion and having teammates introduce their wives by saying, "These are the two guys that cost us the state championship."

Do you want to be in that position? It's tempting to "yeah, but" this ques-tion. "Yeah, but everyone's doing it." "Yeah, but it's tradition." "Yeah, but there's nothing else to do." "Yeah, but I'm not the one taking the drugs—it's them."

Those excuses don't cut it.

In my work with half a million students since 1990, I've heard hundreds of stories of how drugs and alcohol have negatively impacted individuals and teams. I could write an entire book on the stories students have shared with me.

The Effects Are Bigger than You Think

Often the most popular drug used in schools today is alcohol. Some people tend to think alcohol isn't a drug because there's a legal drinking age whereas marijuana, cocaine, LSD, heroin, and other drugs are illegal—no matter how old you are. Whether you—or someone on your team—is using alcohol, marijuana, or steroids, they're all illegal. The detrimental effects of alcohol on performance are well documented and include impairment of the following:

- Balance and steadiness
- Reaction time
- Fine and complex motor skills
- Information processing
- Speech
- Decision making

These are the immediate results of alcohol. There are also these long-term results:

- Legal problems
- Addiction
- Involvement in a traffic accident
- Engaging in risky sexual behavior that may spread disease
- Decline in general health

How Drugs Affect Your Team

What are the potential side affects of drugs and alcohol on the team? If people are using drugs or alcohol it could affect:

- Team spirit

- Momentum

- The image of the team

That's not all. A division between those using and those not using could occur, which could destroy your team's sense of teamwork. Athletes could get caught and be suspended or removed from the team.

So what do you do if you're a captain, you don't use drugs or alcohol, but you know of team members who do? I think

you'd agree, this is a tough question. However, it's a question you to need to think about answering. My recommendation is to have a conversation with your coach on how to handle this situation. There is not a simple answer to this problem. The goal is to create a pact with your coach and teammates on what will happen if someone decides to drink alcohol or use illegal drugs.

Remember, being a captain is not a popularity contest. Being drug and alcohol free isn't going to be an easy task. However, by committing to abstain from these dangerous decisions, you will certainly have a season to remember instead of one you wish you could forget.

Choose Wisely

A wise high school coach of mine once said, "You have the rest of your life to drink if you choose. You only have one chance to participate in high school athletics." I'll never forget that statement. It was right on target, and our football team took it to heart.

On the first day of summer football practice, our coach challenged the team to be drug and alcohol free. He said our team had the potential to have an awesome season. A number of the players on the previous season's team drank a lot of alcohol. Our team knew alcohol played a role in the previous year's poor record and dismal performance.

Our senior season was going to be different. We were not going to let alcohol wreck our potential. That first day of practice, twenty-two seniors and ten juniors pledged to be drug and alcohol free. I'm proud to say, everyone on that team lived up to their word. We went six and two that season, and we went to the playoffs. It was an incredible season, one I will never forget. Had our team fallen into the tradition of alcohol, I honestly believe we would have had only an average season. It certainly would not have been a season of significance.

Even though that was a long time ago, I often reflect on that fall. We were a bunch of young men committing to each other and then playing our hearts out on Friday nights.

"You have the rest of your life to drink. You only have one chance to play high school athletics."

During a pre-season meeting, stand up and present a pledge for teammates not to use drugs and alcohol. If the sport you are a leader of has a tradition of using drugs and alcohol, this is the year to turn it around. By committing to being drug free, you are eliminating one big thing that could keep your team from doing the best that it can.

Student's Pledge

As an athlete, I agree to abide by all rules regarding the use of drugs. I understand that drug addiction is a disease and, even though it may be treatable, it has serious physical and emotional effects—effects that would hurt me, my family, my team, and my school. Given the serious dangers of drug use, I accept and pledge to follow all rules and laws established by my school, team, and community regarding the use of drugs. These include the rules listed in my school's student and athletic handbooks and any other rules established by my coach.

To demonstrate my support, I pledge to:

1. Support my fellow students by setting an example and abstaining from the use of illegal drugs.

2. Avoid enabling any of my fellow students or teammates who use these substances. I will not cover up or lie for them if any rules are broken. I will hold my fellow students and teammates fully responsible and accountable for their actions.

3. Seek information and assistance in dealing with my own or other students' problems relating to drugs.

4. Be honest and open with my parents or guardians about my feelings and problems.

5. Be honest and open with my coach and other school or community personnel.

Student _____

School Name _____Date _____

** PARENTS OR GUARDIANS: We ask that you co-sign this pledge to show your support.

Parent/Guardian _____Date _____

Parent/Guardian _____Date _____

Reprinted with permission from *The Coach's Playbook Against Drugs*, published by the Office of Juvenile Justice and Delinquency Prevention (OJJDP), Washington, DC.

"

Drugs and Drinking

"It seems in our culture that if a person (needs to) drinks by themselves, it's called a problem. If a group (needs to) drink, it's called a party."

—John Crudele

"Drugs take you further than you want to go, keep you there longer than you want to stay, and cost you more than you can ever pay."

—Chester Brewer, Jr.

"The best thing for me and other athletes is to stay out of trouble."

—Shaquille O'Neal

CAPTAIN'S CLIPBOARD

The Effects of Drugs and Alcohol

The immediate effects of alcohol include impairment of the following:
- Balance and steadiness
- Reaction time
- Fine and complex motor skills
- Information processing
- Speech
- Decision making

The long-term effects of alcohol include impairment and:
- Legal problems
- Addiction
- Involvement in a traffic accident

- Engaging in risky sexual behavior that may spread disease
- Decline in general health

If your teammates are using drugs or alcohol it could affect:
- Team spirit
- Momentum
- The image of the team
- Teamwork (creating a division between those using and those not using)
- Team performance (athletes who get caught could get suspended or expelled)

PART 3

GO!

CHAPTER 8
Setting the Tone

If you've ever been to a live concert featuring your favorite singer or band, you know the tone is set the second the lights go down and the entertainers walk out for the opening song. Captains are also tone setters. Every time you walk into a team meeting, practice, or competition, you have the opportunity to set the tone. Will the tone you set be one that lifts others up or will it cause others to turn and walk away? Great captains understand they set the tone before practice, during practice, on the floor of competition, and off. The following ten keys will help set a positive tone and develop a sense of playing beyond the scoreboard.

Key #1: Show Up Every Day

Showing up is not about attendance. Showing up is about being tuned in and focused on the task at hand. It's easy to let your thoughts drift. When that happens important instructions or advice can be missed. It's vital to be mentally present.

Average teams believe they can just mentally show up for the important contests. Rarely does that work consistently. Sure, some teams have pulled it off by getting totally focused at the end of the season around tournament time. Attempting to show up only for the important matches usually backfires as old habits creep in and destroy the team's progress. Captains who show up every day create a strong habit that will carry them throughout the season and throughout their lives.

Key #2: Have Integrity

As an eighth-grade track participant, I was recruited to be the line judge for the long jump competition for a varsity track meet. My job was to watch the line, and if a jumper's foot touched the line or went beyond it, I was to yell out "scratch." Scratching erased the jump.

Our varsity team had an incredible jumper who usually took first place in this event. After the first two jumps, T.S. was in  third place. On his final approach, he clearly stepped over the line, so I yelled, "scratch." For some reason the judge didn't hear me and started to measure his jump. I approached the judge and said T.S. had scratched just as he announced the jump at 22 feet, six inches. That would have been a new school record and he would have taken first place that day.

The jump was not counted. T.S. was going to take third. A few seconds later, T.S. was in my face. He verbally tore into me. "You just cost me the school record, punk!" he yelled. "Why did you do that?" That's the polite version of what happened, and it caught me off guard. I was almost speechless. The only thing I could say was, "You scratched. You went over the line."

That experience has been etched in my mind ever since then. T.S. was willing to have his name on the record board despite the fact he didn't earn the honor. That tells me that he had little honor. T.S. wanted to claim something that wasn't his. Arthur Calwell once said, "It is better to be defeated on principle than to win on lies." If you're going to be a great captain, you have to be honest and have integrity even when no one is watching.

Key #3: Remember: All Eyes Are on You

Whether it's your teammates, the coach, or the people in the stands, everyone is watching you. And they watch you even closer when difficult situations arise. If the official makes a bad call, do you lose your composure, stomp your feet, roll your eyes, and let out a huge sigh for everyone to hear? Do you yell at the official? If you do, how can you get upset when a team-mate does the same thing?

You are the example! Believe it or not, young children watch your performance from the stands and often imitate your responses when faced with the same situation. *You can't get what you're not willing to give.* Make sure you are constantly asking yourself, "Would it be productive if everyone on the team took the same attitude and behavior I'm currently demonstrating?" If the answer is no, it's time to rethink and demonstrate the attitude and behavior of a top-notch leader.

Key #4: Decide to Speak Up or Shut Up

Do you have something to say or do you just have to say some-thing? Too many leaders simply talk too much. Their mouth never stops moving. It's important to communicate, but too much talking can be a turnoff to the team. Pick your words wisely.

If a teammate had a terrible performance, gauge your response after the game or contest. It may be appropriate to talk with that person and try to verbally encourage the person immedi-ately. In other cases, it may be best to just leave the person alone for a day and then give them some supporting words.

Deciding when to speak up or remain silent is a lot about trial and error. No doubt you will mess up and occasionally say the wrong thing to a coach, co-captain, or teammate. When that happens, go to the person, address the situation, and then move on.

Key #5: Appreciate Everyone's Role

Not everyone on the team is going to be a star. Some people may be on the team because it's the only positive thing in their life.

One of my best friends in high school averaged 15 points a season in basketball. He lived for warm-ups prior to the game. While he wasn't talented on the floor, his sense of humor carried the team a long way. He was quick with a joke and could make anyone smile regardless of the situation. He was the spark plug of the team despite the fact he didn't play very much. His role was to provide comic relief.

As a captain, it's vital to support players at all levels. Remember: athletes develop at different rates. A lanky junior can turn into a whole new player as a senior. If you demean ability, you are driving a wedge between you and your teammates. If you're going to play beyond the scoreboard, respect each person's role on the team. Whether they bring out the water or earn the highest score on the beam, respect everyone's role.

Key #6: Smile

The Mayo Clinic released a multi-year study in January 1999  reporting that people who consistently lived with a positive outlook and smiled a lot lived an average of 20% longer. Your attitude and demeanor may help you live 15 years longer!

Have you ever noticed some people who appear to have never smiled in their life? I mean if they were to crack a smile, their face would crumble. Think about it. Do you really want to be around someone who is constantly wearing a scowl on their face? No way.

Effective captains approach games and practice with a smile on their face. Does that mean they are always jumping for joy the first two weeks of practice? No. It means they recognize their attitude is contagious.

Try this as a fun experiment. Smile all day long when you see people and observe their response. Typically you will find they will smile back. It's almost impossible to not smile back when someone smiles at you.

Think about young children. Their laughs are infectious. They start to smile and you immediately do the same. I'm not talking about that stupid grin we sometimes think is a smile. I'm talking about the smile you put on Saturday night when your friends are waiting for you out in the driveway. You have a new pair of jeans on, the hair is where it's supposed to be, and you feel good. As you walk by a full-length mirror, you catch a glance at yourself and back up to take a look. Then the big smile appears on your face and you point to yourself in the mirror and say, "Oh yeah!" That's the smile we need to wear consistently. Try it, and you will see the results.

Key #7: Be Up when Others Are Down

Have you ever been on a team when every-thing starts out wonderful? People are get-ting along, the team has a strong winning record, and everyone is healthy? If you have been a part of a team like that, it's easy to be upbeat and positive. It takes no effort at all during these times.

What happens when the opposite is occurring? You are losing nearly every contest, people are mad because they are not getting enough playing time, and a team star has an injury. Now what? This is the time for a team leader to step up. The team needs you the most at this time.

Obviously you won't be able to turn everything around overnight. You can continue to apply the principles in this book and try to find the silver lining in the cloud. I'm not sug-gesting you jump for joy and act like you are on your way to a state championship. I am suggesting you continue to play beyond the scoreboard to keep working hard and enjoy the process as much as possible. Maybe it's time to plan a fun activity with the team after practice or on the weekend. Maybe you suggest that the team go to a movie or arcade together. Try to find a way to have some fun despite the current situation.

Key #8: Keep Losing in Perspective

Professional basketball coach Phil Jackson once said, "We never let winning go to our head or losing go to our heart." This is a powerful statement to live and play by. After a loss, it's natural to be mad and disappointed. It's all right to hold on to that for a short time. It may serve as motivation to work harder in practice for the next game.

Unfortunately, however, many individuals and teams hold on to the loss way too long. *The only thing you can do after a loss is learn from it. Evaluate what went right and what went wrong.* After you've done that, move on and begin preparations for the next contest.

On the other end of the spectrum, avoid totally blowing off a loss. I've seen teams who lost by a huge margin laugh out loud as to how bad they were beaten. That sends a poor message to the coaching staff and to the fans who are trying to support the team.

Key #9: Keep Winning in Perspective

Remember what Phil Jackson said about winning? Never let it go to your head. It happens almost every season to one team in your school. That team is destroying opponents left and right. Suddenly the team is ranked in the state poll. Then all of the sudden, a team with very little talent comes along and defeats that state-ranked team.

Why does this happen? Usually because players on the team got a little too arrogant and forgot how hard they worked to create their positive result. It can also happen when a team has beaten another team for years. Arrogance is dangerous. Your job as a team captain is to keep the team confident but not arrogant. There is a huge difference. Confidence is believing you are going to win while arrogance is believing you can't be beat. If arrogance creeps into your team, don't be surprised if the team you looked past, sneaks up and beats you.

Key #10: Know the Hazards of Hazing

Hazing is a hot topic with athletic teams. Many upperclassmen believe hazing is just a team tradition, and it should continue because they had to go through it when they were younger. When hazing comes up in my live sessions, I ask anyone who has been hazed if the person enjoyed the process. Almost everyone says no. Most hated being humiliated. Then I ask, "If you hated it, why would you do it to someone else?" It's a difficult question for students to answer. Usually they say "It's tradition."

There is a difference between a team tradition and hazing. Hazing usually scares people and rarely creates cohesion. Traditions support the team and its members and can create unity. Traditions can be something the team has done for years that is fun and not humiliating to it's new members. Instead of hazing, consider developing some strong team traditions. Examples might include dressing up during the school day for games, chanting a cheer, attending a team meal, having team breakfasts, or showing up at a movie together. Some teams donate their time to community service by adopting a highway or putting on a sports clinic for younger kids. In a community adjacent to mine, there is a go-cart racing track. The go-carts can hit up to 40 miles per hour. Talk about a good time. These traditions would not be considered intimidating or humiliating.

Hazing is a serious issue. Alfred University in New York State released a survey indicating 48 percent of high school students who belong to groups report being subjected to hazing activities. Hazing is defined as "any humiliating or dangerous activity expected of you to join a group, regardless of your willingness to participate." Example of hazing in the study included shaving heads, taping people to trees, or stripping a student down to his underwear and locking him out of school during a weight lifting session. Sometimes hazing results in a student's death.

In many states, hazing is not only unethical, it's illegal. People who participate in hazing an individual have lost their student privileges, been suspended from school, and even kicked off the team.

Hazing is like a container of rotting egg salad in the refrigerator. You don't want to open it because you know the smell will knock you to the floor. Throw it in the garbage before it gets legs of its own. If your team has encouraged hazing in the past, it's also time to throw it in the garbage and begin positive traditions that will last for years.

Here's a unique spin on hazing. Informally tell your teammates from the youngest grade to meet at the practice field or gym at 7 a.m. sharp with their tennis shoes on. Don't tell them what's going to happen. Then show up with bagels and cream cheese for everyone. Talk about tossing out hazing and developing a strong team tradition. Try to think of something that will bond a team together on and off the floor of competition. By adopting team traditions instead of practicing hazing, you are putting yourself in a position to have a season to remember.

I remember a team bonding experience as a senior during football season. There was an older gentleman in his eighties who lived across the street from our practice field named Jack. He always hung around the practice field and was quick with a joke and knew all of the varsity player's names. Everyone enjoyed seeing Jack around the field. He was our unofficial coach.

In the middle of the season, Jack suddenly died. It was a real downer for our team because we had grown accustomed to seeing his big smile and quick wit. On the day of his funeral, the entire varsity team went to his funeral with our game jerseys on. While it was a sad day, it was cool to see all of Jack's friends and relatives smile when the team walked into the church for his final tribute. That day had a major impact on every team member. We're only on this earth for a short time so we might as well enjoy life and each other.

Great concerts, just like great sports seasons, set the tone to create unforgettable memories. By applying the strategies in this chapter you will no doubt create a bank full of them.

Winning

"We generally make too much of winning. Let's face it, someone always has to win: that is the nature of competition. But the mere fact of winning doesn't make you great."

—Wilt Chamberlain

"History has demonstrated that the most notable winners usually encountered heart-breaking obstacles before they triumphed. They won because they refused to become discouraged by their defeats."

—Bertie Forbes

"In the end, it's extra effort that separates a winner from second place. But winning takes a lot more than that. It starts with complete command of the fundamentals. Then it takes desire, determination, discipline, and self-sacrifice. Finally, it takes a great deal of love, fairness, and respect for your fellow man. Put all these together, and even if you don't win, how can you lose?"

—Jesse Owens

"A winner never whines."

—Paul Brown

"We all like to win, but enjoy the moments along the way, no matter the outcome. Just put your heart and soul into it, and give 110%. If you do this, you will always be a winner to the person who counts most...you!"

—Marlene Blaszcyk

Losing

"I can accept failure. Everyone fails at something. But I can't accept not trying."

—Michael Jordan

"Most games are lost, not won."

—Casey Stengel

"I've always made a total effort, even when the odds seemed entirely against me. I never quit trying; I never felt that I didn't have a chance to win."

—Arnold Palmer

"Enjoy the success that you have, and don't be too hard on yourself when you don't do well. Too many times we beat up on ourselves. Just relax and enjoy it."

—Patty Sheehan

Winning and Losing

"In life we choose whether or not we want to be a winner or a loser. To be a winner, we must devote time and hard work. To be a loser, you do nothing, and that's exactly what you will get, nothing."

—Patrick Boles

"There is no doubt in my mind that there are many ways to be a winner, but there is really only one way to be a loser, and that is to fail and not look beyond the failure."

—Kyle Rote, Jr.

continued...

"

"I've always tried to do my best on the ball field. I can't do any more than that. I always give one hundred percent: and if my team loses, I come back and give one hundred percent the next day."

—Jessie Barfield

"The winners in life think constantly in terms of I can, I will, and I am. Losers, on the other hand, concentrate their waking thoughts on what they should have or would have done, or what they can't do."

—Denis Waitley

"

CAPTAIN'S CLIPBOARD

Keys to Setting the Tone

- Show up every day.

- Have integrity.

- Remember: All eyes are on you.

- Decide to speak up or shut up.

- Appreciate everyone's role.

- Smile.

- Be *up* when others are down.

- Keep losing in perspective.

- Keep winning in perspective.

- Know the hazards of hazing.

CHAPTER 9

Managing Conflict

Have you ever noticed how it's easy to be upbeat and excited when your team is performing at a top level? Teammates are laughing and smiling. They enjoy being around each other. Coaches may knock a few minutes off of physical conditioning because the past four matches have gone extremely well.

Then out of nowhere, something new and uncomfortable pops up. Suddenly your teammates are intentionally not passing you the puck. Teammates start to laugh and whisper in each other's ears as you stretch out before swim practice. Maybe a loss sends your coaching staff off the deep end. The coaches verbally rip your team apart, and a few players are considering quitting in the middle of the season. Now what?

Inevitable Conflicts

You've just experienced a pitfall called conflict. How will you work through this and come out stronger? This is one area I had a difficult time with as a team captain. I'm one of those individuals who doesn't like conflict. Too often I tried to ignore the crisis and hoped it would go away. Occasionally, that works. But most of the time, it doesn't.

This chapter is going to give you some ideas on working *through* conflict. You will learn a formula to manage conflict in a tactful manner instead of losing your cool and saying things you may regret later. You will become a stronger individual and a stronger team because you had the courage to face the conflict and resolve it.

This chapter is titled managing conflict. It doesn't say ignoring conflict or attacking conflict. Let's face it. *Conflict is inevitable.* If you put two or more people in a room together, it won't take long before a problem arises. If a problem is addressed in an assertive fashion, you and your team will be able to tackle the issue and move on. If it's not addressed appropriately, the conflict could snowball into a major crisis that divides the team and eventually leads people to leave the team. Then you find yourself losing games you shouldn't have because of off-the-court issues.

I've heard hundreds of horror stories about how conflict has destroyed teams and friendships. Sometimes the conflict or problem is the reason why the relationship was destroyed. But many times, it's the way people attempt to resolve the conflict that's the bigger issue.

Dealing with Conflict

Most people deal with conflict in one of two ways. They let the problem go without addressing it or they wait until they are so irritated by it that they blow up at the person involved in the problem. Neither of these approaches works very well.

Unfortunately, we get little information on dealing with conflict constructively. I attended twelve years of school and four years of college with a major in business and a minor in speech communication, and I never had a course or even a conversation on dealing with conflict. We typically deal with conflict based upon the authority figures in our lives. Authority figures may include parents, stepparents, neighbors, coaches, and teachers. If no one taught them effective strategies of conflict management and they handle conflict in a poor fashion, we could continue the pattern by default.

The ideas in this chapter have literally changed my life. I have gone from a person who would avoid conflict like a vicious disease to someone who is comfortable with conflict. That still doesn't mean that I like conflict. But I'm more comfortable with conflict because of the distinctions I've learned.

Start Right

What's the best way to deal with a conflict? Too often people think you should address conflict as soon as it happens—no matter where you are. If you have a problem or conflict with a teammate or coach, do you bring it up in front of a large group or while the whole team is watching? No! At least not at the beginning. Could there be a time when several people want to address the issue and the only way to do that is in the presence of the entire group? Sure. But think about a time when you had someone jump on your case in front of a large group. Did you feel comfortable or uncomfortable? It's an uneasy feeling having a group stare at you while someone is in your face about an issue.

If you've ever been in a store and witnessed a married couple start to argue with each other, you'll see some funny things. Complete strangers will stop just to hear these two people yell at each other. People get a weird kick out of watching arguments. You don't want or need others in the middle of a conflict.

The best way to approach conflict is to create a one-on-one situation. Tell the person that you want to talk privately. It's a lot easier to create a comfortable atmosphere when only two people are involved.

The Right Tone

Now think about your tone of voice. Have you ever read a note from a friend and thought, "How dare they say that." You interpreted the meaning with a certain critical or negative tone in your head. You've probably talked back to your parents, and they responded with, "Watch your mouth."

Maybe you responded in the way most teens have done in this situation. You responded in a much different, positive tone saying, "What? All I said was...." Then you smiled and thought you had talked your way out of it. You've done that haven't you? The tone of your voice plays a major role in dealing with conflict.

What kind of tone should you have? It's better to be *curious* not *accusatory*. If you approach the person like a detective who is humbly trying to figure out a problem, you will have an excellent chance of having the other person open up so the two of you can deal with the situation. Getting in someone's face and yelling in a harsh voice, "What's your problem?" will not work. When you resort to force, it usually comes back. When you fight fire with fire, you just get a bigger fire. Fight fire with water because that will put it out. By taking a curious tone you will be able to put out the fire of conflict and preserve your relationship.

The OTFDN Formula

The formula that has had such an impact on my approach to dealing with conflict well is the acronym: OTFDN. When I give this formula in a live session, I present it in a mnemonic device, which is a unique story that incorporates the letters in the formula.

When you were in elementary school music class, you had to learn the line notes of EGBDF. Your instructor probably had you

remember these lines by saying, "Every Good Boy Does Fine." It's been several years since I was in elementary school, but I still remember that mnemonic device.

The mnemonic device for dealing with conflict is easy to remember by thinking: *Open The Front Door Now* (OTFDN). When you think of those words, they create a picture in your mind about opening the door and addressing the problem in a tactful fashion.

Once you know the effective tone of voice and you've found a private place to discuss the problem so it's just the two of you, it's time to use the "O" in the OTFDN formula.

"O" stands for observation—Let's say a teammate has been late for practice the past three days. This is frustrating for the coaching staff and the rest of the team. It's not respectful nor is it promoting team unity. Now it's time to address the problem.

You might say something like, "I've noticed that you've been late for practice the past three days." You're stating what you have seen or observed. This is an assertive way of addressing the problem. It's not threatening nor is it a timid approach.

"T" stands for thoughts—The next part of the exchange might sound like this, "I'm *curious* to get your thoughts on that." Why do you want to get this person's thoughts on the issue when that person is creating the problem? You may not have all the facts. Maybe that person knows something you don't know.

Have you ever had someone verbally attack you without giving you a chance to explain your side of the story? That is a pathetic approach. It's vital to get the person's thoughts on the issue because it will determine where you go next.

If the teammate says, "My parents are at work, and my grandpa's medical aide is on vacation so I've been running home to make sure he gets his medication," you're going to back off and take a softer approach. That explains why your teammate has been late.

If the teammate says, "Yeah. I know I was late. I was just talking with some friends, and the time got away from me." This excuse doesn't cut it. By asking for the person's thoughts in a detective-like fashion, you are attempting to figure out what is going through this person's head regarding the problem or situation. Now it's time to use the "F" in the formula.

"F" stands for feedback—At this point you get a chance to give your feedback on the situation. Explain how this person's actions are affecting you or the team. If the teammate had said he was racing home to help a sick grandparent, you might say, "Wow, I wished you would have told me. What can I do to help?" The feedback you give shows your concern for your teammate and his situation.

If the teammate had said he was just talking with some friends, proceed with caution. This is delicate. You don't want to rip into the person, yet you don't want to dance around the issue. Give the feedback, as you would want it given to you—in a fair, calm fashion.

In this situation, you might say, "I just wanted you to know that everyone on the team including myself is frustrated by your late arrival. It looks like you don't respect the coaches or the people who are there on time."

After you covered the feedback phase, the two of you probably will talk some more. This feedback should shed some light on the person's actions. Often, people have no idea how their actions affect others. When you're finished giving each other feedback, move to the "D" in the formula.

"D" stands for desire—Clearly state what you want to change. It may sound something like, "I really want you to show up on time so that we have a great practice from start to finish."

Watch for the person's response. If the person is nodding in agreement, move to the "N" in the formula. If you sense the person disagrees with you, go back to the observation phase and continue the conversation.

"N" stands for next time—Once the two of you agree on what needs to change, lay the groundwork for the next time this situation arises. If the teammate was late because he was taking care of a sick parent you might say, "The next time you have to get home right after school, please tell me so that I can pass along that information to the coach."

If you're dealing with the teammate who was late because he was just talking with friends, you might say, "Next time this happens, the coach may not let you start the game." Use the phrase "next time" because it lays out the consequence if the person repeats the offense.

This formula works in a variety of situations. Let's say your coach has been rude and difficult to be around for the past few days. Approach your coach after practice and use the OTFDN formula. Say something like, "Coach, you don't seem to be yourself the past few days. You've been ranting and raving a lot, and I just wanted to get your thoughts on that." By taking this assertive approach, almost every coach will give you an explanation about what's going on.

Mediating Conflict

As a team leader, it's your obligation to be a conflict manager. Throughout the season, challenges will arise that require your

mediation. This isn't easy. It's tempting to just ignore the conflict with the hopes it will disappear.

Don't let small issues build until they get out of control. If you have a problem with a coach or teammate, be strong enough to address the situation. Do it as soon as possible. Remember: you may not have all the facts. You could be making an unfair or inaccurate conclusion based upon the limited knowledge you have.

Although the OTFDN formula is effective, it is not 100%. Sometimes you can't work through the conflict, but at least you had the courage to try to resolve it. Team leaders are wise enough to understand that sometimes people are going to disagree. But you can come to an agreement on that. Agree to disagree.

Sometimes both sides will see the other's point of view but neither will compromise their position. You can still have a season of significance even if everybody doesn't agree all the time. It's rare to have complete harmony on a team.

I promise the OTFDN formula will help you manage conflict in a positive manner. You will be able to use this formula not only with teammates and coaches but in every relationship you have. Conflict is inevitable. Manage it and then move on!

"

Conflict

"Obstacles are challenges for winners and excuses for losers."

—M.E. Kerr in *Gentlehands*

"I like pressure. If I'm not on the edge of failure, I'm not being sufficiently challenged."

—Jewel

"Don't get mad, get better."

—Cindy Bristow

"

CAPTAIN'S CLIPBOARD

Conflicts Are Inevitable

Use the OTFDN Formula:

Observation

Thoughts

Feedback

Desire

Next Time

CHAPTER 10
The Art of Sportsmanship

If you've ever watched an artist begin a painting, you'll notice the design is first created in the artist's head and heart. Then it appears on the canvas. Most artists visualize the big picture

and then start working one area of a canvas at a time. That's how artists create masterpieces.

The same principle can be applied to sportsmanship. It's created in the heart and head then appears by the performance on the court, field, or floor. Great teams understand the big picture regarding sportsmanship.

Our whole world is suffering from poor sportsmanship, not just in athletics. Drive down a freeway and watch people respond when they get cut off or when someone needs to make a lane change in order to reach an exit. It's amazing to see the finger gestures and anger that occur over basically harmless acts. Airlines are battling air rage where passengers waiting for a late flight become violent towards airline employees. Schools are seeing more students in the classroom verbally blow up after receiving a bad grade. In short, we need to commit to sportsmanship on and off the floor of competition.

But what is sportsmanship? If you ask one hundred people, you would probably get as many responses. *Usually sportsmanship boils down to playing by the rules, accepting the official's calls, and committing to being a class act regardless of the outcome of the game.* This is a life skill. This book is about playing *beyond* the scoreboard and understanding that the experiences and knowledge you are gaining right now will become a launching pad to the future.

There are several areas of sportsmanship. Unfortunately, some of these areas you have little control over. These include the behavior of opponents, fans, and opposing coaches. It's nearly impossible to *control* other people's behavior. However, you can *influence* their behavior. There is little you can do to influence the opponent's sportsmanship, but you can choose how you and your team responds and reacts to various situations.

Sportsmanship is committing to be a class act regardless of the circumstances. This is a skill you can use for the rest of your life. People who are class acts gain admiration from others. They draw others in. They look at the big picture regarding their approach to life and their sport. They don't get too high with their success or fall apart when they face failure.

The following five keys to sportsmanship will prove to be vital as you pursue a season of significance.

Key #1: Cool heads prevail

Key #2: You can't control a bad call

Key #3: The other team is the opponent, not the enemy

Key #4: Arrogance is ugly

Key #5: Win or lose, commit to class

Key #1: Cool Heads Prevail

How many times have you witnessed an athlete completely lose it? A hot-headed athlete rants and raves about a call or becomes unglued over an opponent's remark or gesture. The player then says something inappropriate that rattles the team, coach, or fans. As a result, a technical foul is issued. If this behavior continues, the athlete is removed from the game.

Captains must keep their cool despite the urge to explode. In Richard Carlson's book, *Don't Sweat the Small Stuff,* he talks about being the eye of the tornado. The eye is the center of the tornado, and it's totally calm. The winds may be gusting at a hundred miles per hour, but the eye remains calm. Great leaders focus on staying at the eye of the tornado. They understand that losing their "cool" will not help the team.

Key #2: You Can't Control a Bad Call

Officials are human. They will make mistakes every now and then. Although you can't control a bad call, you can control your *response* to a bad call. Making a weird face, rolling your eyes, or shaking your head in disbelief will never reverse a call. What's done is done. Deal with it and move on without any cynical comment. If you fall into the trap of questioning every call that has been made, you will start to lose focus on your performance and your game plan.

Key #3: The Other Team Is the Opponent, Not the Enemy

It's easy to get caught up in the hype of a rivalry and start to believe the other team is the enemy. They're not. The other team is your opponent. This is an important distinction. Competition is great when it brings out the best in us.

However, if you have a long history of playing against a squad and it hasn't been a friendly exchange, sometimes teams begin to act like they would do anything to destroy the other team. When this happens, it can get ugly in a hurry.

Key #4: Arrogance Is Ugly

Have you ever competed against a team that gave you the impression they were going to destroy you without any effort at all? Maybe members from the other team came out of the locker room, smirked, and made smart-aleck comments at your team during warm-ups. They act like the game was over before it even started.

If you've ever competed against a team like that and won, you know the incredible feeling of taking those players down a notch or two. At the moment of victory, it's tempting to give them a taste of their own medicine, maybe smirk back or make some retaliatory comments as you are shaking hands after the game. *Don't do it!*

Commit to being a class act. Don't do the very thing you despised in the first place. Players on the other team know how they acted. They probably feel stupid now that they lost. (As they should.) In a situation like that, top-notch teams shake hands and celebrate in the locker room.

Key #5: Win or Lose, Commit to Class

Keep winning and losing in perspective. Let's say you're playing a team twice in a season. The first game was played in your high school, and you won. After the game, you and your teammates pumped your fists with joy and pointed to the scoreboard to rub in the final results.

When you visit your opponent's school the next time you play them, you may be setting yourself up for a disaster. Those players will remember how you acted. If you lose, the other team and its fans will most likely make a huge deal about the win. Keep a win in perspective. Enjoy it. Then start to prepare for the next match up.

Sportsmanship and Officials

When interviewing several officials, I discovered a number of insightful input about sportsmanship. I think you will find this information important and useful throughout the season.

- **Mistakes can happen.** As I mentioned earlier, no one is perfect. That includes officials. They're going to make mistakes from time to time. Their goal is to call a game or match in a fair, consistent manner. Normally, they are officiating because they enjoy working with teens and still want to be a part of a sport. If you are expecting them to call a perfect game, you're setting yourself up for disappointment.

Officials admit they are going to miss a call. Sometimes those calls will be in your favor, sometimes they won't. It usually balances out in the end. Keep the mistakes in perspective and control the things you can control.

- **Be respectful.** It's important to watch your attitude and behavior toward officials. I asked several officials this, "If a team has an arrogant attitude and is disrespectful, does that play a role in how you call the game or match?" Every official I interviewed said basically the same thing, "It shouldn't, but it could." In other words, your personal conduct and attitude plays a role in how officials see the game. So how do you show respect to an official?

- **Watch your mouth.** Officials grow tired of players questioning every call or letting out a loud sigh after a call has been made. It's best to just keep quiet after a call even if you disagree with it. If someone needs to question a call, it's best if a coach does it.

- **Know the rules.** If you truly understand the rules of the game, you will have a lot more credibility with the officials. If you ask them an uninformed question, they may start to wonder how much you really understand about your sport. Get the rulebook and take time to go through it.

- **Know when and how to ask questions during competition.** The officials I interviewed gave me several key pointers on asking questions. The first one is to know the difference between a judgment call and a rule interpretation call. A judgment call could include unsportsmanlike conduct, an offensive charge in basketball, or whether gymnastic leaps were at a medium or superior level. You will have little or no chance in convincing an official to change this type of call. You may learn something by asking how the official saw the event, but it's rare to see an official reverse a judgment call.

A rule interpretation is different. It could include why a receiver became ineligible to receive a pass after going out of bounds or why a base runner on first is automatically out if the ball is popped to an infielder. If there was a mistake made by an official on a rule interpretation call, there is a chance the call may be reversed. The key is to fully understand the rule. If you feel confident in your knowledge on a rule interpretation call, you may respectfully approach the official and ask for permission to ask them a question.

The best way to ask a question is to approach an official when he is not involved in another task. Ask, "Is it okay for me to ask you a question?" Make sure your tone of voice is positive.

If it's an appropriate time, the official will usually allow you to ask the question. Then you might say something like, "I thought the rule was…" and then state your case. The official will explain his reasoning behind the call. If the official was wrong, he could correct the decision. Typically, a call won't be reversed, but the official's explanation will tell you something about how he will be officiating the rest of the contest.

Every official is different. One set of officials may be strict with the rules while others may "let you play." The best teams adjust and play their hearts out regardless of the officiating.

• **Volunteer to be an official.** One of the best suggestions officials gave me about helping high school athletes learn more about officiating is to volunteer to referee or judge a middle school scrimmage or game. It's a surefire way to see what officials are going through. You will have an opportunity to hear the moans and groans from the audience and watch the players react to your calls.

A famous NFL television commentator was known to be critical of officials during his broadcasts. He was invited to take part in the official's boot camp. He figured he would probably teach the officials something.

Needless to say, this experience completely changed him. He was amazed at how difficult it was to be in the middle of the action and try to call a fair game. Now when he's in the broadcasting booth, his comments on officiating are different. He is more supportive of official's calls even when the instant replay showed the official made a mistake. Take an opportunity to be an "unofficial" official, and see what you can learn. I promise it will be an eye-opening experience.

Sticky Situations

Sportsmanship is easy to demonstrate when the path is smooth. What happens to you and your team when you run into a difficult or sticky situation? Coaches and players have shared a number of sticky situations with me through conversations and surveys. A sticky situation is a circumstance that arises where it isn't clear what to do. Usually there are many options, and typically there isn't one right way and one wrong way.

Take a few moments and read through each of these sticky situations, which really happened. Think about how you would respond if you were faced with the same set of circumstances.

- **Sticky bus situation**—On a bus trip back to your school after a loss, one of your teammates tosses a glass container out of the window. Everyone—including the coach—hears the crash. The coach, who is very upset, stands up and asks who is responsible for the bottle. No one takes responsibility. You're not sure who is responsible, but you know the team will pay a price if no one confesses. What do you do?

- **Sticky attitude situation**—A teammate constantly has a bad attitude. Everything is a major pain in the neck for this individual. When something goes wrong, she complains to anyone who will listen. Unfortunately, others listen, and her attitude is rubbing off on others. What do you do?

- **Sticky temper situation**—A key player has a short temper. His "hot head" has resulted in unsportsmanlike penalties a few times. His temper and actions seem to rattle the team and coaches. What do you do?

- **Sticky theft situation**—While competing in another town, one of your teammates steals a wallet or purse from the locker room. You appear to be the only one who witnesses the theft. What do you do?

- **Sticky teammate situation**—A teammate consistently questions the officials' calls. This appears to agitate the officials. It's a close competition. The results of a technical foul could be the difference between a victory and a loss. What do you do? When do you do it?

- **Sticky rival situation**—You just lost a close one to your biggest rival. As you shake hands, players on the opposing team verbally rub it in that they won. What do you do?

- **Sticky social situation**—One of your teammates seems more interested in the social part of being on the team than committing to having a great season. What do you do?

- **Sticky coach situation**—Your coach completely becomes unglued and loses her temper after a loss. She uses foul language in a dramatic way. The coach berates almost every member of the team. What do you do? What is the best approach? If you chose to talk about the situation, who do you talk to and when?

- **Sticky rumor situation**—A vicious lie is being passed about you concerning a violation of a team rule. Your teammates seem to act differently around you. You feel it is affecting the team and the coaching staff. What do you do?

- **Sticky alcohol situation**—It's a fact. A teammate was drinking alcohol. This person has consistently been a top performer. He denies he's drinking. What do you do?

- **Sticky star situation**—One of your teammates is more concerned about personal statistics than in team results. The rest of the team is growing tired of this person's approach. Some team members decide to take it upon themselves to ensure that the star doesn't get the stats she wants. You can see the division starting to rip the team apart. What do you do?

Life-Long Sportsmanship

Sportsmanship doesn't stop after graduation. As you get into the workforce, it will continue to play a role in your life. You will face countless situations where you will have to choose to follow the ideas in this chapter and commit to being a class act or throw the ideas out and let the urge to strike back rule.

It's your choice. I hope you take a positive sportsmanship approach in all areas of life.

This page left intentionally blank

Sportsmanship

"Every time you compete, try harder to improve on your last performance. Give nothing short of your very best."

—Elgin Baylor

"Sports can do so much. They've given me a framework: meeting new people, confidence, self-esteem, discipline, and motivation. All these things I learned, whether I knew I was learning them or not, through sports."

—Mia Hamm

"Part of being a champ is acting like a champ. You have to learn how to win and not run away when you lose... Everyone has bad stretches and real successes. Either way, you have to be careful not to lose your confidence or get too confident."

—Nancy Kerrigan

CAPTAIN'S CLIPBOARD

Five Keys to Sportsmanship

Key #1: Cool heads prevail.

Key #2: You can't control a bad call.

Key #3: The other team is the opponent, not the enemy.

Key #4: Arrogance is ugly.

Key #5: Win or lose, commit to class.

PART 4

INSTANT REPLAY

CHAPTER 11
A Look Back

The season is over. But your role as a team captain is not. It's now time to take a quick look back at the season and prepare for the end of the season banquet or celebration. It's important to continue your leadership role until all the final details are wrapped up.

Start by evaluating the season. The next page has a few questions for you to consider. Take time to answer these questions since your answers may be helpful for compiling your final thoughts for your banquet. If your team has never had a banquet, start a tradition and plan one. It's a great way to bring closure and allow the players on your team to celebrate all their accomplishments.

A Look-Back Survey

The High Point of the Season
The Low Point of the Season
The Surprise of Your Season
I'll Always Remember
The Lessons I learned this Season Include

Appreciate Your Coach

Most coaches are underpaid and under appreciated. They put in countless hours and dedicate themselves to their team. They deal with critics and unsupportive people all the time. Many times, their family life suffers during the season because they're not home as often as they would like to be.

The end of the season is a great time to show your appreciation for your coach. It's easy to think that coaches coach for the money. But it isn't true. They coach for the love of the sport and the enjoyment they receive from working with teens. Are there exceptions? Of course. However, if your coach went the extra mile this year, make sure he or she knows about it.

A friend of mine coaches a girl's Nordic skiing team in Minnesota. This coach understands the power of playing beyond the scoreboard. The team just finished a miserable season in regards to wins and losses. They only won once during the entire the season. Despite the team's record, however, the girls had fun, learned a lot about life and the value of teamwork.

As the team captain took the microphone for her parting words during the end-of-the-season banquet, she handed her coach a wrapped box. Inside was a quilt that was sewn together by each team member. Each girl had designed a square. The message this coach received from this quilt was the team had a season of significance. The quilt was a symbol of thanks for coaching the team beyond the scoreboard.

As the coach told this story to me, his voice quivered with emotion. He said, "I'll never forget that team." I'm confident that quilt will always be in his house. He will probably show it to his grandkids some day.

What could you do to show your coach your appreciation? Maybe it's something you create or something you purchase. It doesn't have to be expensive to be meaningful. If each player contributes five to ten dollars, you can figure out a gift that will be remembered. A great time to present this gift is at your team banquet.

Another great act of appreciation is to write your coach a letter. Everyone can write something. Or one person on the team 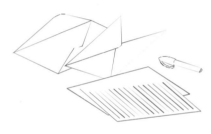 who has a knack for writing can write the letter and have everyone sign it. These letters are seldom thrown out. Usually, they go into a box of coaching memories. In addition to the team letter, I would encourage you to write a personal note to the coach expressing your gratitude.

Average captains blow the whole appreciation thing off. But you're not an average captain! Take the time to wrap up the season on an upbeat note, regardless of the team's record.

Enjoy Your Experience

Being an effective team captain is easier said than done. However, I am confident that you have the ability to lead your team to an unforgettable season. Playing beyond the scoreboard is an approach you can use for the rest of your life.

You are creating a path to the future by being a team captain today. Enjoy the season. Enjoy your teammates. Most of all, enjoy the experience of being a team captain.

I poured my heart and soul into putting this book together. Hopefully, you have enjoyed reading it as much as I enjoyed writing it. Now, go out and *Play Beyond the Scoreboard* and lead you team to a season of significance!

"

Your Season of Significance

"Sports do not build character, they reveal it."

—Heywood Hale Broun

"The most important thing in the Olympic Games is not to win but to take part, just as the most important thing in life is not the triumph but the struggle. The essential thing is not to have conquered but to have fought well."

—The Olympic Creed

"Sports challenge you and build character for everything you do in life."

—Howie Long

"

CAPTAIN'S CLIPBOARD

Three Ways
to End
Your Season Well

1. Evaluate your season.

2. Appreciate your coach.

3. Enjoy your experience.

APPENDIX 1
Resources

If you're serious about leadership, the following books will be a great help.

> *How to Step Up as a Teen Leader & Still Keep Your Friends* by Craig Hillier (Lakeville, MN: Winning Edge Seminars, 1997)
>
> *Teen Power* by America's top youth speakers (Lakewood, CO: ChesPress Publications, 1996)
>
> *Lead Now or Step Aside* by America's top youth speakers (Lakewood, CO: ChesPress Publications, 2000)

These three resources are available from Winning Edge Seminars, 10968 203rd Street West, Lakeville, MN 55044; (952) 985-5885; (800) 446-3343; email: WinningE@aol.com; www.craighillier.com.

21 Irrefutable Leadership Laws by John C. Maxwell (Nashville, Tennessee: Thomas Nelson Publishers, 1998)

Awaken the Giant Within by Anthony Robbins (New York: Fireside, 1993)

Becoming a Woman of Influence by Carol Kent (Colorado Springs, Colorado: NavPress, 1999)

Chicken Soup for the Teenage Soul series by Jack Canfield and Mark Victor Hansen (Deerfield Beach, Florida: 1997, 1998, 2000)

Developing the Leader Within You by John C. Maxwell (Nashville, Tennessee: Thomas Nelson Publishers, 2001)

Life Strategies for Teens by Jay McGraw (New York: Simon & Schuster, 2000)

The Seven Habits of Highly Effective Teens by Sean Covey (New York: Fireside, 1998)

Success Is a Choice by Rick Pitino (New York: Broadway Books, 1997)

The Winner Within by Pat Riley (New York: G.P. Putnam's Sons, 1993)

Team Captain Calendar/Planner

Simply put, this is the best planner you will find. It's designed specifically for teens and team leaders. This resource will help you stay on top of your school schedule as well as your team events. It's filled with powerful quotes and useful leadership information. Contact: Gary Halvorson, Coaching to Change Lives, 218 Plainview Drive, River Falls, WI 54022; (715) 386-6871; email: ghalvor@spacestar.net.

APPENDIX 2
FUNdraisers

It's always nice to have a few extra dollars in your team's account. Every state and every school have different policies regarding fundraisers. Before you dive into a fundraiser, check with your athletic director on what kind of fundraiser your team can do and where the proceeds will go. Many times, teams can have their own special account for various fundraisers. These extra dollars can go for uniforms, camps, or a team trip. The possibilities are endless. Feel free to adapt the following ideas to fit your sport. The key is to make sure they are *fun!*

Sports Clinic

Advertise a clinic for the younger students in your community. The coaching staff and players can run the camp. First, decide on the length of the camp. Normally, a three- to five-day time frame works well. Advertise the camp by creating posters and duplicating them for elementary-age students. Deliver the posters to elementary and middle schools in your community. It's a low-cost, low-risk idea that can provide some serious dollars for your team. It also gives the younger kids a chance to interact with the varsity athletes. Speaking from experience, my kids love attending these clinics. When they attend the varsity games, they remember the players who helped them at camp.

Host a Tournament

Team tournaments are held for a variety of sports nearly every weekend. Why not host one? Your school probably has the facilities to make it happen. First, seek permission from the administration. Check into the liability of hosting such a tournament. Think about how you are going to run concessions. Search out area teams that may have an interest in participating. Decide on a reasonable amount of money required to participate in the event. Keep in mind, however, that hosting a tournament is a big project. It typically takes at least three years before a tournament takes in big dollars. There is a girl's basketball team in the Minneapolis area that now takes in $24,000 a year from the two-day tournament that the team hosts.

Lift a Thon

This may not work with all sports. However, give it a shot and see what you can accomplish. A lift a thon is basically a weight-lifting contest. You can decide on the different type of lifts to use. Examples include the bench press, dead lift, clean and jerk. Teammates go door to door with a schedule for the season and give a free invitation to the lift a thon. They also can ask community members to donate money, such as a penny per pound lifted. Some people donate even more. Hold the event in the high school gym. Make sure there is music playing in the background with an announcer telling the audience who is lifting and the type of lift the person is attempting.

Couch Potato

In this idea, a lucky winner in a drawing gets to watch a game from the best seat in the house. Here's how it works: Locate a comfortable couch (the owner of a furniture store might donate one if the store is given enough recognition). Depending on the event, position the couch on the sidelines or in the stands. (Some schools actually have a platform specially built for the couch.) Students then sell tickets prior to the game, usually 50 cents per ticket or three tickets for a dollar. On the day of the game, you draw a ticket to declare a winner. The winner and a guest get to sit on the couch for the entire game. Some schools even have one couch for students and one for adults. You could even sweeten the pot by also giving the winner $10 to spend at the concession stand. Maybe a faculty member delivers the items from the concession stand so the winner doesn't even have to get off the couch to stand in line! It's pure profit and pure fun.

Dash for Cash

My friend Phil Boyte submitted this idea. It is similar to a 50-50 raffle. Prior to a game, collect dollars from people who want a chance to dash for cash. Give each participant a ticket and put the matching ticket into a can. This can holds all the tickets you will draw from later. At the game's half-time break, take half of the money collected and put it away for your profit. Lay out the other half on the court or field. Spread the one-dollar bills about three feet apart to make it a challenge for the person to pick them up. Draw a winning ticket from the can and give the ticket holder 30 seconds to dash for cash and pick up as many dollars as possible. Consider providing a carpenter's bag for the winner to store the cash. As soon as the thirty seconds expire, the remaining dollars are collected for your additional profit.

APPENDIX 3
Inspiring Sports Quotes

Sometimes having the right words at the right moment can make a huge difference. Maybe you need to give yourself a boost as a team captain. Maybe your team needs to hear words of inspiration and hope.

Throughout this book, you can find quotes on different aspects of being a team leader and a team player. Use those quotes and the ones in this chapter as a theme for the week or something to share before a game, match, or competition. They also could be used for a team T-shirt. If so, remember to give the individual credit by printing his or her name next to the quote.

Keep on Trying

During different parts of your season, you and your teammates may get discouraged. Maybe you're tired. Maybe the season is dragging on too long. You may want to quit—or take a break. Use these quotes to remind you to keep going, even when things aren't going well.

"We all have days when we just don't seem to have the energy or the interest in working out at peak effort. These are the times to reach inside ourselves and try to find that extra oomph that will motivate us."

—Kara Leverte Farley and Sheila Curry

"Don't throw in the towel. Use it for wiping the sweat off your face."

—Unknown

"I never gave up, even when people told me I'd never make it."

—Bob Wickman

"The ones that want to achieve motivate themselves."

—Mike Ditka

"If you aren't playing well, the game isn't as much fun. When that happens, I tell myself just to go out and play the game as I did when I was a kid."

—Tom Watson

"It's a rough road that leads to the heights of greatness."

—Seneca

Take Risks

It's easy to do the same thing over and over again when you know it works, but sometimes you need to take a risk. Use these quotes to encourage yourself to step out of the box and try something new.

"The purpose of any athletic endeavor is to challenge human limits both on and off the playing field."

—Unknown

"Most people run a race to see who is fastest. I run a race to see who has the most guts."

—Steve Prefontaine

"Show me a guy who's afraid to look bad, and I'll show you a guy you can beat every time."

—Lou Brock

"We must either find a way or make one."

—Hannibal

Practice and Play Hard

Everyone talks about the importance of giving your best. It's essential to do this during each practice in addition to the games. Sometimes it's tempting to slack off, but successful athletes talk about the importance of giving their all—all the time.

"To give anything less than your best is to sacrifice your gift."

—Steve Prefontaine

"It's not necessarily the amount of time you spend at practice that counts; it's what you put into the practice."

—Eric Lindros

"How you respond to the challenge in the second half will determine what you become after the game, whether you are a winner or a loser."

—Lou Holtz

"Excellence is not a singular act but a habit. You are what you do repeatedly."

—Shaquille O'Neal

"The vision of a champion is someone who is bent over, drenched in sweat, at the point of exhaustion when no one else is watching."

—Anson Dorrance

"The game isn't over till it's over."

—Yogi Berra

Remember the Big Picture

Sometimes you and your team can get so focused on a specific play, game, or technique that you'll lose sight of the big picture. Take a step back. Think about your entire season. Think about your entire team. Take another step back. Consider what this is all about in regards to your entire life.

"Before I go out on the field every day, I tell myself, 'You are having fun, and you want to set a good example to those who are watching.' "

—Cory Snyder

"In wheelchair sports, people thought athletes with disabilities were courageous and inspirational. They never give them credit for simply being competitive."

—Jean Driscoll

"I know that I'm never as good or as bad as any single performance. I've never believed my critics or my worshippers."

—Charles Barkley

"Do you know what my favorite part of the game is? The opportunity to play."

—Mike Singletary

Keep Learning

Even athletes with the best skills and the most experience can learn more. Maybe it's another skill, another technique. Or maybe it's another idea that will help the team play more in sync with each other. Playing beyond the scoreboard means continuing to learn more and to try new things.

"The best and fastest way to learn a sport is to watch and imitate a champion."

—Jean-Claude Killy

Set High Expectations

Once you or your team has met a goal, then what? Set a higher goal. Stretch. Expect more of yourself and of your team.

> "I've worked too hard and too long to let anything stand in the way of my goals. I will not let my teammates down, and I will not let myself down."
>
> —Mia Hamm

> "Even if you're on the right track, you'll get run over if you just sit there."
>
> —Will Rogers

> "Other people may not have had high expectations for me...but I had high expectations for myself."
>
> —Shannon Miller

I Want to Hear from You!

Got a great story on being a team captain? Would you like to comment on this book? Do you have a picture of your team or team event that you would like me to consider putting on my website? Do you want me to speak to your leadership group or student body?

If so, I want to hear from you. Tell me about:

- How your season went
- How you created team chemistry
- How you overcame a major obstacle
- How this book helped you in being a team captain
- How you created a season of significance

Go to my website at www.craighillier.com and let me know all about it. Or contact me at: Winning Edge Seminars, 10968 203rd Street West, Lakeville, MN 55044; (952) 985-5885; (800) 446-3343. I promise to reply to all of your comments and ideas. Who knows, you may be a part of my next book!

About Your Season

This is your season of significance. Record some information about your season on this page and include a picture of yourself. Keep this book as a keepsake of your season. You'll enjoy looking back at it during high school reunions.

```
┌─────────────────────────────────────┐
│                                     │
│                                     │
│                                     │
│           Your Picture Here         │
│                                     │
│                                     │
│                                     │
└─────────────────────────────────────┘
```

Your Coach(es): _____

_____

Your Co-Captain (if any): _____

About Your Team:_____

_____

_____

About Your Season: _____

_____

_____

_____

_____

NOTES

NOTES

NOTES

NOTES

NOTES

NOTES

NOTES